Rust In Peace

Malcolm Tucker

Photographs from the Michael Worthington-Williams archives

First published 2007

ISBN - 1-85443-225-7
ISBN-13 - 978-1-85443-225-4

Printed and bound in
Singapore by Star Standard

for the publisher

Dalton Watson Fine Books
1 Arundel Court, Elverlands Close,
Ferring, West Sussex BN12 5QE, England

1730 Christopher Drive,
Deerfield, IL 60015,
USA

www.daltonwatson.com

Notes and Acknowledgments

I would like to give a special word of thanks to my editor and publisher, Glyn Morris and my book designer Ben Gibbs; to David Burgess-Wise for sharing his immense knowledge when checking factual veracity; to Nick Georgano for his seminal work *The Beaulieu Encyclopedia of the Automobile*, so often my place of first reference; to the many other authors who have written motoring books that weigh down the shelves of my reference library; to all the enthusiasts, who over the years, have sent photographs to Mike Worthington-Williams, from which I have made my selection; and lastly, the Collis family for allowing access to their tractor collection, from which the images of rusting metal were photographed.

Malcolm Tucker, Hampshire 2007

Contents

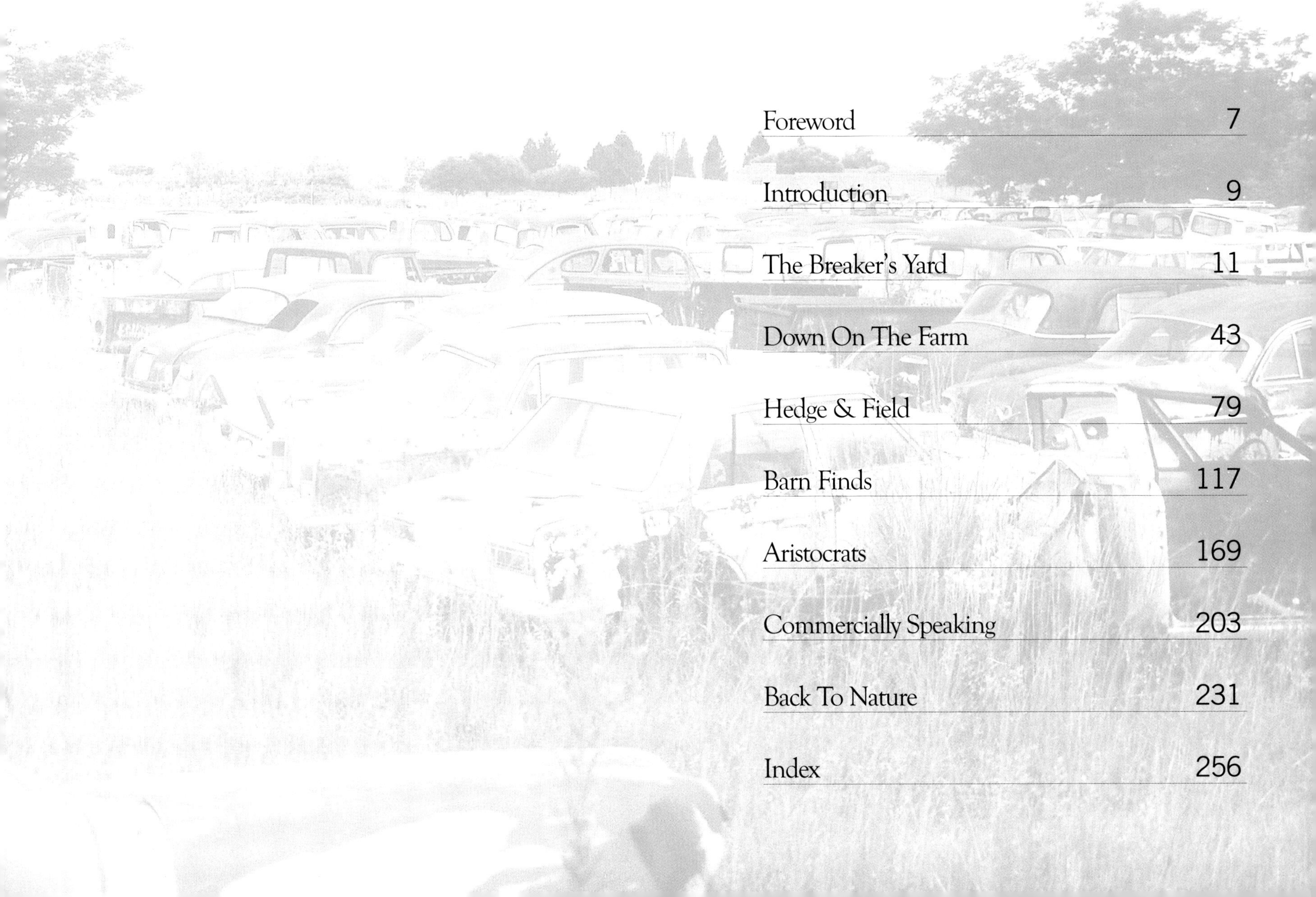

Foreword 7

Introduction 9

The Breaker's Yard 11

Down On The Farm 43

Hedge & Field 79

Barn Finds 117

Aristocrats 169

Commercially Speaking 203

Back To Nature 231

Index 256

Foreword

Back in 1956 I made my first barn discovery – a 1926 BSA 986cc motorcycle taxi combination which had at one time operated on a rank at the Aquarium on Brighton seafront. I duly wrote up the acquisition in *Veteran and Vintage* magazine, and in the fifty years which have elapsed since that time I have reported literally hundreds of discoveries in my regular columns in most of the classic vehicle magazines.

From these finds I have owned examples of Angus-Sanderson, Crouch, Calcott, Horstmann, Trojan, Fiat Tipo 56, Armstrong Siddeley Lonsdale, Morris 10/4 Special Coupé, Morris Commercial, Chrysler Wimbledon, Pontiac turret top coupé, Canadian Pontiac, Austin Seven, Wolseley Ten, Singer Le Mans, Riley Monaco, Crossley Ten Torquay, Riley Kestrel, three Austin Somersets, three Rover P4s, a Rover P5, Singer SM1500 and Austin 20/4, as well as Monopole and SGM motorcycles, many of which were acquired in derelict condition.

When I was a child, both my uncles George and Harry dabbled in second-hand cars, and in those days immediately following World War II, the only available cars for Mr. Everyman were pre-war. Thus all the established scrap-yards were thriving, selling off complete cars which had been dumped with them in 1939, or spares for those cars still in private hands. These cars had been laid up, often in less than ideal conditions, for the duration of the war.

Sadly, the days of the traditional scrap-yard, where a vehicle might lie undisturbed for upwards of forty years, are fast coming to an end as a result of environmental pressures and EU regulations. Nowadays, if a vehicle survives more than six weeks before being crushed, it is exceptional.

Every cloud has a silver lining, and in this case the demise of the traditional scrap-yard has forced car-hungry enthusiasts like myself to search longer and harder in farm and barn, hedge and field, garage and garden, for individual gems of neglected or abandoned vehicles. It is this ever-increasing rarity that makes the remaining motors more and more valuable as time goes by: an unpleasant fact when trying to buy a car needing restoration, but it is that increased value which keeps our motoring heritage out of the crusher.

Traditional scrap-yards remain my spiritual home, and it is typical that, following an expedition to the Orkney Isles in 1985 with my good friend Ted Purcell, and having been asked if I had visited any of the ancient ruins to be found there, I answered, "No, but we did find some really juicy scrap-yards!" Those yards yielded the remains of an 18/50 Bean, a 17/70 Storey, a 1912 Regal Underslung, a V8 Autovia and a World War I Albion lorry, all of which were reported in "Orcadian Odyssey" in *The Automobile*. The yard known locally as "The Camp" had been a barrage balloon station during the Great War.

It has reached the point now, where if a reader of one or other of the several magazines for which I write regularly discovers an interesting vehicle, the first reaction seems to be "I must tell Mike WW!" I long ago ceased to worry that the stream of cars, commercials, buses and motorcycles would dry up and that I would be unable to fill my columns. Every month, and after fifty years, I still have more stories than I can print, and those vehicles illustrated here represent only a fraction of the total of those which have passed over my desk. Long may it all continue.

Mike Worthington-Williams - 2007

Introduction

Derelict and unloved vehicles have an unquenchable fascination for those of us afflicted with an interest in transport from times past. The unrestored barn-find or 'trouvé de grange' as some dealers in such motors would say, will fetch at auction far above its estimate of sensible value. At such events, some sub-conscious or ancient emotion rules our common sense, and the twinkle in the auctioneer's eye grows ever brighter whilst assessing his increasing commission on the sale.

Experienced vehicle owner-restorers know that financial loss may be great, frustration caused by incalculable delays will be immense and distaff disharmony may also be noticeable. We may never purchase another mode of transport that is 'ripe for restoration', but we will never ever stop our eyes widening with an accompanying grin and quickening pulse at the site of an automotive shape in the gloaming of a barn, or the infinite colours of a rust-streaked mudguard protruding from an invasive bramble patch.

The magic of an old car may be in its ability to evoke the memory of days gone by. Once inside, one can so easily imagine friendly roads free of traffic, destinations where excitement was not dampened by worries of parking, vandalism or theft, and the laughter of long-gone loved ones may be a little clearer in the memory. Perhaps it is the human flair for only remembering the past as a happy place. Summers were always sunny and winters were always havens of crisp mornings and powdery snow; untrue of course, for why did our mums buy us raincoats, and did we not catch colds?

Many are attracted to a car used in one's youth, but others may seek a make that was lusted after but unaffordable when new. Now, with cash to spare, that well remembered Bentley, Jaguar or Aston Martin may be within grasp, at least in unrestored condition. Perhaps the attraction is to be away from Eurobox conformity; cars designed by computer with safety, wind resistance, cost of production and operation, being all important. Yes! these cars are infinitely safer, faster and in many cases more comfortable than their predecessors, but they lack those highly desirable qualities of individuality and being designed first and foremost around the human form.

Fortunately, by his life-long devotion to the cause, Mike Worthington-Williams has made it possible for us all to enjoy the discovery of old vehicles. His photographic archive is second to none as a record of abandoned, scrapped, and neglected motors. It is with great thanks to him for allowing me access to that archive, that this book has been possible, but on behalf of all 'old vehicle' enthusiasts, I thank him even more for his lifetime interest in recording the last days, and sometimes saving of so many interesting vehicles.

Malcolm Tucker - 2007

The Breaker's Yard

Chapter One

The Breaker's Yard

The spiritual homes of Mike Worthington-Williams have been called by many names; car breakers, scrap-yard, car wreckers, or vehicle dismantlers. Now, in an age when dustmen are domestic waste logisticians, shop assistants are assistant sales executives, and secretaries are enablers, redundant vehicles go to an 'end of life recycling station'.

Until a few years ago, to wander around such a place may have revealed any number of interesting vehicles. Of course they would be at the edges of the yard, covered by vegetation and miscellaneous scrap metal – long time residents, from which parts had been taken with less and less frequency as time passed by.

Sun, wind and rain would have done their worst to render the remains unusable, but if windows and paintwork were intact then a complete car might well remain in savable condition for many years. European legislation has forced the old-style yards to close, their cars now gone to the crusher. A modern dismantler will keep a vehicle for only a few weeks, what remains is crushed to make way for another day's intake of recyclable material on wheels.

Elephant Motors, Clare's for Spares, Jacombs, Percy Voake's yard at Adversane, Brimfield's, Harris' yard, Willets of Noah's Ark Lane, Buckland's, Gordon Passey's yard, Rush Green Motors, Medlar's and Motolympia to name a few. Most now gone, those remaining, modernised but the spirit of these wonderful mausoleums of motoring metal lives on in the memories of older enthusiasts and of course, photographs.

Right: c.1945 Austin 16 Army Staff Car
Certain models of the 1939 Austin range continued in production throughout the war years, but new for 1944 the 16hp was only the 1939 12hp with a larger 2.2 litre engine. Surrounded by the remains of steam traction engines of an earlier age, the doors and body sides have parted company. No doubt a symptom of the appalling quality of immediate post-war steel.

Left: c.1959 Singer Gazelle Estate
The first Singers designed and built under Rootes Group ownership retained the Singer designed 1.5 litre ohc engine. Later cars used the Hillman Minx ohv engine of similar size. This car is a relatively rare Estate version, which was offered alongside the saloon and convertible.

Below Left: 1930 Jowett Black Prince, 1929 Singer Junior, 1926 Jowett Tourer
All pre-war Jowetts used a flat twin engine of their own design, which gave great torque; a benefit in the Yorkshire Dales of the company's home county. Both these cars had an engine of 907cc. They were sold under the slogan "The pull of an elephant with the appetite of a canary and the docility of a lamb". The Singer, with its 848cc single-ohc engine is an example of the country's third favourite make – after Morris and Austin.

Below Right: c.1950 Jowett Javelin, c.1950 Ford Anglia, c.1935 Standard 10 or 12
The Jowett was an advanced and stylish car for its day. The Ford and Standard offered basic but reliable motoring, but no style at all. All three look to have done their final duty as suppliers of parts, to keep more fortunate sisters on the road.

Page 15: c.1937 Standard Flying 16,20 or V8
Easily identified by its 'Union flag' radiator emblem (missing here) Standard cars were standard fare rather than standard setters. They never quite gained the following of Austin or Morris, their main competition. If this is a V8, it is rare indeed as the 2.7 litre engine was too much for the chassis and brakes. The model was discontinued after a scant two years. Alongside the Standard is something more interesting. Possibly a 1920s Renault, judging by the scuttle-mounted radiators.

Left: A melange of British motors from the '50s and '60s
There are eighteen easily identifiable cars and four, more difficult to name. This could almost be the car park at a point to point event in the late 1960s. Did any of them seduce a classic car restorer?

Above Right: Pre-war radiator grilles
These items were usually made of brass and as such had an immediate value to the car breaker. Period photographs of scrap-yards from the 1920s and the following three decades are often disappointing, as radiator shells and bonnets are invariably missing, making identification difficult.

Right: c.1962 Daimler Majestic
Large formal Daimlers were the choice of Royalty until Rolls-Royce took that honour in the early 1950s. For many decades, smaller models were also manufactured, the Majestic being one such car. It sported a six-cylinder engine of 3.5 litres, disc brakes and automatic gear selection. By now owned by Jaguar, these elegant and expensive cars were soon to be discontinued to avoid competition with the 'Big Cat' saloons. This example slumbers next to a Standard Vanguard Phase 1, of about 1952.

Left: Americans Await
A selection of 1950s American saloons, including Buick, Oldsmobile, Ford and one Packard - the only representative of America's better manufacturers.

Right: 1956 Ford Customline, 1953 Dodge, 1952 Ford Crestline and 1949 Plymouth Special Deluxe
A difficult quartet to identify, the Customline should have the suffix 'probably' added. All of them are from the lower end of the makers' ranges.

Below Left: 1951 Hudson Hornet
Fitted with an up-rated six-cylinder engine of 308-cid, an example of the model won that year's NASCAR championship. What was initially an outstandingly different body style soon became dated. For engineering reasons and a lack of capital, the small independent Hudson company had to make the best of the aging design. Just how many acres can an American scrap-yard cover?

Below Right: 1936 Hudson
An earlier example of the make, but already showing a leaning towards an almost Art Deco design.
This could be a straight-six or eight engined car. Judging by the British Motor Corporation's front wing to the fore of the picture, the Hudson was one of the many assembled in Britain at the company's Great West Road, London depot. Although substantially complete, nature has rendered this imported colonial best left to the photographer's lens.

Above Left: c.1948 Hillman Minx, c.1949 Vauxhall Velox

Both these cars were interim models, basically re-worked pre-war designs. The Hillman with its four-cylinder engine and the Velox with its six really did not offer the new-car buyer of the late 1940s much to get excited about. Looking for all the world like an audience at an outdoor Shakespeare festival, these tired and tiered cars await a short future.

Below Left: c.1961 Standard Vanguard Series III Luxury Six

Restyled in 1956 to gain its suffix, Vanguards were becoming long in the tooth. Some twenty six thousand were built as the Vanguard Vignale, featuring the tried and tested four-cylinder 2 litre engine. The more powerful car's six designation referred to the number of cylinders. Less than ten thousand examples left the factory.

Above Right: c.1959 Sunbeam Rapier

A Rootes Group offering of a more sporting two-door saloon, the dark painted side flash shows this to be a Series III version. Its compatriots are also probably the same series, but undoubtedly Sunbeams.

Below Right: c.1957 Austin A35 Van, c.1955 Austin A40 Cambridge, c.1959 Singer Gazelle

The A35 was derived from the A30, Britain's first small car to feature stressed-skin unitary construction. The Cambridge was the first British car to have a 'woman colour consultant' employed to help the designers. The Gazelle, another Rootes Group offering, used the same body shell as the Sunbeam Rapier.

Left: c.1951-57 Vauxhall E-Type Velox
These seven cars look to be all examples of the mid-range 2.25 litre six-cylinder engined Velox, although the line might contain the lesser four-cylinder 1.5 litre engined Wyvern, or the deluxe Cresta variant, which shared the six-cylinder unit. Whatever the collective noun is for Vauxhalls, this fine row has weathered in a climate kinder than our own.

Right: c.1957 Alfa Romeo 1900 Coupé
Known as the Super Sprint model, this Pinin Farina bodied car was capable of nearly 120mph. This example rests in South America, where humidity is no friend to an abandoned classic.

Below Left: 1939 Ford V8 Fordor Series 91A
The last year for Ford to place the headlights between radiator and wing, later cars saw the lights moved out to the curve of the wing. Bonnet side vents and chrome trim were unique to this year. The location is unknown, but judging by sun, lack of rust, and right-hand drive, this is probably an Australian or New Zealand graveyard.

Below Right: c.1950 Jaguar MkV
Seen resting alongside the South American Alfa Romeo, the first new Jaguar model after WWII, has been stripped of most of its brightwork and has suffered the attention of Latino vandals.

Page 24: Australian Choices
Too many to name. A selection of local Utes, large Americans and British stalwarts cover the bush. Close inspection shows a few BMC products.

Page 25: 1948 Buick Super
A typical example of Harley Earl's 'rubenesque' styling, this convertible was mid-range between the Special and Roadmaster models. Buyers of the day were fiercely loyal to their chosen make, even from father to son. The wide open spaces of America make searching a 'wrecking yard' a mammoth task.

Above Left: c.1952 Humber, 1938 Buick Roadmaster, c.1948 mystery American and c.1959 Ford Lowline
The Humber might be a Hawk, Super Snipe, Pullman or Imperial. The Buick features a straight-8 Dynaflow engine and coil suspension. The Ford is a Consul, judging by the trim, it was the least expensive of the Consul, Zephyr and Zodiac triumvirate.

Below Left: 1947 Buick Sedan
Little changed for the 1947 model year, as 1949 would see a new model range. Part of this car's 'gun sight' mascot is missing, although it retains most of its brightwork. With an English Ford and a Chrysler Valiant in the photograph, it is possible that this is another 'Down under' location.

Above Left Page 27: 1947 Ford V8 Coupé
Just like Buick, the Fords of this period were made over '42s. Various body styles were offered, but these delightful little coupés remain as gentle on the eye as they were when new. Cheaper straight six's were available, the whole range making Ford the biggest sellers that year. That could be an early 1950s Mercedes 300 keeping the Ford company.

Below Left Page 27: International Hearse
With little to go on with which to date this American vehicle, it would appear to have a style from the mid 1930s. International were mainly builders of commercial vehicles, well known for sturdy pick-up trucks. A few were converted to passenger vehicles by outside coachbuilders. This hearse has a magnificent roof ornament, somewhat akin to the British Coronation coach.

Right: 1946 Buick 8

Buick returned to post-war car production with a 1942 design, of which this is a mildly face-lifted example. So acceptable was it, that they stretched things out until the 1950 model year. There were many versions; this is probably a Super. Enjoying the sun, the verdant grass would suggest a Southern State for this resting Buick. It looks eminently restorable, being free of serious rust and also complete.

Above: in France?

An early post-war Mercedes 170, petrol or diesel engined, jostles with a Ford model Y from around 1935, possibly from Ford's Parisian factory at Asnières, which is separated from the Citroën Traction Avant by another Ford Y. A blue sky and Charente style roof tiles make South-West France a likely setting for these close companions.

27

Left: Rads for sale
Looking mainly undamaged, these grilles were once the proud identification for a Wolseley, Daimler, Austin, MG and Chevrolet.

Below Left: 1933/4 Austin 7 Sports 65
Produced for only two years and more generally known as the Nippy, these delightful little sports cars were, as their name suggests capable of 65 m.p.h. With the occupants' backsides a mere 14 inches from the ground, the impression of speed was exhilarating. This car, challenged by gravity and corrosion was rescued and restoration is underway.

Below Right: c.1938 SS Jaguar
Offered with 1.5, 2.5, and 3.5 litre engines, these saloons were carried over to post-war production, until the MkV arrived in 1949. SS stood for Standard Swallow, a reference to the Standard cars on which the earlier models were based and Swallow sidecars, which was William Lyons' first transport venture. In 1945 the SS part of the name was dropped for obvious reasons.

Right: c.1952 Humber Hawks
The Humber in the page 26 photograph is revealed here to be a Hawk. The roof of its sister has suffered the irreparable fate of the mechanical grabber. How many otherwise restorable classics have been scrapped due to the same few seconds of hydraulic pressure?

Left: c.1955 Wolseley 4/44 or 6/90,
c.1963 Humber Vogue Series I, c.1962 Jaguars
Taken on a winter's day, the scene looks more like
the car park at Miss Haversham's wedding, than a
British car breakers.

Above: Settled in Shropshire
All small family cars from the 1950s and '60s,
all are probably past hope; except perhaps the
early '50s white Austin A30/A35 (far right).
The Austin A30/A35 retained the rounded Austin
look longer than any other model, being replaced by
the Mini in 1959. The oldest car here is probably
the Ford Prefect (behind the Austin), a model that
was superceded in 1954.

Right: c.1955 Standard Vanguard
This, a Phase II version had lost the bulbous beetle
back of the 1947 Phase I. The II was offered with
the proven 2 litre petrol engine or a 2.1 litre diesel
unit; the first British car with an oil burner. Sun and
only surface rust suggests this is another New World
resting place.

31

Left: c.1933 Ford V8
Technically, these three cars could have been fitted with Ford's four-cylinder engines, but by sheer volume of V8 units produced, that is much more likely. Solid as Excalibur in the stone and with plenty of power from the unburstable 3.6 litre engine, these cars were good for a few decades before gaining a new lease of life as hot rods.

Below Left: Car wall
It was not unusual for 'scrappies' to erect a fence made of cars and parts, to dissuade the ever threatening thieves that are attracted to such environments.

Below Right: c.1934 Morris 8, c.1934 Citroën
This and the preceding two photographs were taken at the same Canary Islands compound. The Morris is a Series I, judging by its spoked wheels. The Citroën's double chevrons show it to be post 1933, and one of the Rosalie range. The bonnet in the foreground might well be a Ford and the GC registration number seems to grace a very '30s Austin-looking boot.

Above: Encore á France
Photographed in Depanauto, France in 2001, this pre-war hoard will quicken the heart of many a restorer needing that 'special' part. Note the chassis frames leaning against the wall.

Right: c.1953 Austin A40s
Unusually, both these cars have the optional factory fitted sun roofs.
Sold as Austin Somersets, they joined the manufacturer's other 'county' cars – Hampshire, Devon, Dorset and Hereford. Possibly more by luck than judgment, the design was rust resistant and lasted longer than other makes of the period.

Left: 1933 Buick sedan
Restyled in 1931, with a range of straight-eight engines, the '33 cars were offered as model 50, 60, 80 and 90. The engines were good enough to see Buick through to 1952. Although Bonnie and Clyde drove a Ford to their deaths, this car is similar enough in design to encourage the trigger-happy locals to have customised it accordingly.

Right: 1953 Packard Caribbean Coupé
John Reinhart's 1951 redesign of the cumbersome post-war cars was well received. Although it was the sort of thing that would become known as a 'chrome barge', they are highly sought after by today's collectors. By no means past redemption it is hoped that this example has found a loving owner.

Below Left: c.1936 Packard 120 Series
Following the depression, Packard bought out a cheaper model to join their established quality products. Named for its chassis length in inches, the new car was a tearaway success and did much to keep the business in the black. Another similar car lurks behind, both seemingly having donated many parts to more fortunate siblings.

Below Right: 1936 Ford Fordor
An unusual radiator grille for Ford in this year. Note the modified bumper and bonnet air vents. A possible rebuild, but more likely a perfect basis for a custom car. It is surprising that no one has relieved the burden of those V8 hubcaps.

Left: c.1957 Standard 8 or 10
Designed to compete with the Morris Minor and Austin A30,
the small Standards were not that successful. The 8's were very
basic, originally having no external boot lid, wind-up windows nor
hub caps. The 10's had a larger engine and a few more creature
comforts. A saloon balances on top of a rarer estate version which
was sold as the Companion.

Right: Belgium Bean Feast
In a secret location near to Brussels lies this cache of recent
classics. Most appear in good, if neglected condition. One can
only hope they are released onto the market before deterioration
of the cars or their owner reaches the point of no return.

Above: 1929 Austin 7 Saloon
Beloved by all and driven by many, Austin 7s such as this are nearly
always restorable in some way. This one will surely receive a re-created
sporting body of some sort and a second lease of life. The body shell of
a MkII Austin 7 Ruby sits behind.

Above Left: 1930 Willys Six
Willys are of course best known for mass production of the American
Bantam Company designed WWII Jeep, but car manufacture had
started in 1914. The success of this model, new for 1930, was hampered
by the smaller Willys Whippet; a successful competitor to Ford's Model A.

Below Far Left: c.1949 Austin Sheerline
Austin's first completely new post-war model was designed to be a cheaper
alternative to the Rolls-Royce or Bentley. Although a large Austin had been
a perfectly acceptable 'thrifty' alternative in the '20s and '30s, the post-war
buyers were mainly hire companies and official bodies. This one saw
sterling service for the Mayor of Melbourne, before the slow descent to a
fixed abode with pastoral views.

Below Left: c.1952 Jowett Javelin
Powered by a flat four ohv engine of 1500cc, the streamlined integral body
was designed by MG's Gerald Palmer. All this, plus advanced steering and
suspension made the Javelin a good car. They did well in events such as
the Monte Carlo and Tulip rallies. For all its modernity, the picture shows
the Javelin still had rear hinged front doors.

Right: c.1934 BSA 10hp Peerless Coupé
These small BSA cars were really a slightly cheaper version of their
Lanchester siblings. They used a side-valve engine as against the
Lanchester ohv unit. An evocative shot with a winter's mist rising,
the tree has almost certainly grown to accommodate the car.

Left: c.1935 Vauxhall Light Six D Series
Another 'down under' car, this drophead coupé, possibly with dickey seat would have been a fine car when new. Probably not a commercially viable restoration project – but when did that ever stop us?

Below Left: 1926 Hupmobile A1
Located in Brentwood, South Australia, this example of a good quality vintage American has lasted well. New for 1926, the six-cylinder car was better received than the much vaunted straight eights of a year earlier. This was solely due to price, the larger car being just as well-built as the smaller.

Below Right: c.1949 Ford V8 Pilots
These British Fords were a post-war rehash of the earlier American Model 62. The 3.6 litre engine made them fast cars for their class, although the styling was hardly cutting edge. The New South Wales weather has caused a deal of rust, but strangely not to the chromium lamp-bodies.

Right: New Zealand in 2001
The recent photograph shows an array of mostly British BMC/Leyland products, with a couple of notable Americans to the fore, both Dodges from the early 1940s. The manicured lawns of this yard are probably due to grazing sheep.

Down On The Farm
Chapter Two

Down On The Farm

Old vehicles take up space, and at one stage of their lives become unsightly and worthless. Few of us have the space or desire to keep such redundant items, except farmers, of course; for they never throw anything away, however unlikely that it may be of future use.

The fortunate vehicles, agricultural, commercial or private will have been pushed under cover, hopefully away from the corrosive effects of avian droppings. The less lucky ones will slowly decline, out of sight and out of mind in a quiet corner of farmyard or field.

This chapter deals with those cars resting around the farm buildings. Doubtless the intention is to restore them one day, or at least move them. But life on the farm being what it is, animals, fields and the man from the ministry need immediate attention; which may just be the reasons why these motors have lasted so long.

As with the breaker's yards, time marches on, and modern mechanised and enlarged farms need to maximise their use of space. Abandoned vehicles in muddy yards have to make way for properly surfaced and drained areas. It is now the small farm or smallholding where these cars survive into the 21st century.

Right: 1935 Austin 10/4 Lichfield Saloon
This was the first model year for the 'new look', more curvaceous, with the painted radiator grille used for the whole range from the little 7 Ruby to the massive 20 Mayfair limousine. An 1125cc engine and a wheelbase twelve inches longer than the Ruby made this the ideal family car. Languishing next to an early Mini, this Ten-Four was probably too much of a family pet for the farmer to scrap. No doubt his rose-tinted specs show it in better condition than seen here.

Above Left: 1930 Austin 12/4 Burnham Saloon
Just scraping in as a 'vintage car' (1919-1930), the earlier Twelve-Four had a reputation for being as near to indestructible as a car can be. Many of them attained extraordinary mileages, some with an appalling lack of servicing. Not only were the mechanicals good, but so were the Austin-built bodies. Simply designed but well constructed. New to the fresh air, this car was about to undergo restoration and a new life.

Below Left: 1929 Austin 16/6
Similar coachwork to the preceding car, but with the deeper radiator surround. As the model name suggests, this car had a six-cylinder engine. The Sixteen designation refers to the convoluted British tax 'R.A.C rating' of 15.9hp. In truth the 2249cc unit produced 36bhp. Out on a spring day after a long period off the road, this would seem to be another car destined for better things.

Below Right: 1937 Austin 12 Ascot Saloon
This year saw the penultimate iteration of the pre-war Austin, with a lower wider look. The Ascot was offered in this form and as a cabriolet; the opening, cloth part of the roof being above the door frames, as with the Citroën 2CV. Even as late as 1993, when the photograph was taken, it was quite likely for such a car to be crushed or put to the torch.

Right: 1954 Austin Somerset
Austin's new post-war range of family cars was launched in 1948, when the pre-war designed 8,10,12 and 16hp models were dropped. The replacements had names such as Devon, Dorset and Hampshire. In 1952, the 1200cc engined A40 Devon was completely restyled and named A40 Somerset. It and the larger A70 Hereford and smaller A30 had a distinctive styling, most aptly described by one elderly lady as "the car that looks like a tomato." Retaining its delicate diecast grille and other brightwork, the best this car could hope for would have been as a parts donor and a slow decline to oblivion.

Below Left: 1952 MG TD
With a string of small sporting two-seaters produced before the war, MG were set to 'export or die' as the government of the day prompted. The TC model started production in 1945, and was a massive influence on the British sports car boom in post-war America. The model was updated for 1950 with revised suspension and steering. The package was further enhanced by subtle changes to the bodywork. Showing its 1200cc four-cylinder engine with twin SU carburettors, this TD looks settled for the duration.

Below Right: 1951 Alvis TA21 saloon
The great name of Alvis had been responsible for the definitive 'Post-Vintage Thoroughbreds' of the 1930s, with the Speed 20, 25 and 4.3 litre models. Post-war, the company produced more mundane, but equally appreciated cars. The 3 litre TA21 produced 93bhp. Most of the closed bodies were made by Mulliners of Birmingham and the open ones by Tickfords. Severe frontal impact has rendered this car suitable for retirement. The twin evils of post-war steel and farmyard neglect have hastened the process of returning to nature.

Right: c.1947 Austin 10
In 1939, Austin had brought out a new range, that featured a curved chrome and painted radiator shell, onto which closed an 'alligator' style bonnet.
Until the arrival of the freshly designed Devon and Dorset in 1948, this look would have to do. In fairness they were quite neat and well balanced.
Neat is not the word for this example. Eaten by rust it would soon be in more parts than those from which it was made. Hopefully the farmer did not think he had a piece of valuable motoring history.

Above: c.1946 Wolseley 18/85 Series III
Offered for 1938, the model was re-introduced in 1945 and lasted for another three years. Latterly, a badge-engineered Morris; the Series III was not as good as the earlier pure Wolseley models. With its six-cylinder engine, it was a good choice for a wealthy farmer. Having gone beyond economic restoration, neglect and partial dismantling have made this the perfect home for free range chickens.

Left: 1931 Standard Little 9 Saloon

22bhp from a 1005cc engine gave the Little Nine modest performance, although the engine was 33% larger than the Austin 7s, and developed power was greater than the most sporting 7s on offer. Fully laden with a family of four and their luggage, this and similar cars of the era made slow progress towards the annual seaside holiday. In 1989, this car changed hands for £200. Restored, it would have made an endearing contribution to any 'classic' car show.

Above Right: 1935 BSA 10hp

Never as popular as Austin, Morris or Ford, these 10hp cars were in fact manufactured by Lanchester. As such they should have had more quality appeal than they did. An 1185cc side-valve engine gave adequate performance for the time, but the overall design was too 'average' to make the cars outstanding. The body has survived fairly well, but it's doubtful this example from the Birmingham Small Arms Co Ltd ever took the road again.

Right: 1934 Standard 10 Saloon

The next step up on the Standard ladder, from the Nine, was this 1343cc engined offering. By this year, the roofline had become a little more rounded, but chromium plate had yet to find its way onto the headlamp bodies. A somewhat forlorn but savable example, it is shown close enough to the roadway to be at risk from vandals. The blue cover would suggest that this was home for the car.

Pages 52 & 53: c.1967 Riley Elf Saloon, c.1965 Morris 1000 Traveller, c.1958 Austin A35 Saloon

The Elf was a brave attempt to offer the Austin/Morris Mini buyer something a little more luxurious, with a leather and walnut interior and an extended boot. They never made a real impression on the market. The Traveller was perhaps the most popular offering in the well-loved Minor/1000 range, despite its propensity for wood rot. Its Austin stable mate, with which it shared an engine was BMC's post-war effort of the 7hp. One can almost feel the cold damp day on which this photograph was taken.

Left: c.1966 Jaguar MkII
Found in Blackpool, this is one of the later versions with thinner bumpers and plastic upholstery. The engine size and therefore model designation it bears is not possible to determine. Careful examination will show ample proof of the rust, to which these cars were prone in later life. The urban backdrop is perfect for the 'car on bricks'. How long did the window glass survive?

Lower Left: 1940 Vauxhall 10
In 1937, Vauxhall bought out its first range to use chassis-less Integral Construction, the 10hp being the smallest of the models. Revamped for December 1945, the main body section was even carried forward to the 'new' look Wyvern and Velox range of cars in 1948. Flat tyres sunk into mud establish this as a long time roadside inhabitant. Its overall good condition must surely mean the roadway is private, away from the attention of destructive youths.

Lower Right: c.1952 Ford Prefect
This, the larger of the 'sit up and beg' small cars, had a 10hp motor. In this guise it was the most attractive of the Popular, Anglia, Prefect triumvirate. They soldiered on until replacement in 1953. Many tired examples were used as a basis for kit-built sports cars with glass fibre bodies; the 1172cc engine being suited to mild tuning. A working life now past, this farm car waits beside a Fordson Major E27N Tractor. The bicycle is still in use.

Above: c.1958 Triumph TR3A
The Triumph TR range were true sports cars, second only to the MG in the eyes of the early 1950s motoring public. The TR3A used the ubiquitous 1991cc four-cylinder engine from the Standard Vanguard which in 100bhp form was good enough to propel the sports car to over 100mph. Later versions became increasingly more civilized, which is a polite way to say softer, heavier and thirstier; all attributes to make a true sports car into a touring car. With its factory fitted 'centre lock' wire wheels and optional hard top, this car is almost complete and damage free. Some suburban passer-by must surely have rescued her by now.

Left: c.1958 Austin Healey 100/6, c.1958 MGA
The 'big' Healey was a favourite in America as well as its home country. A brute force basher, it was heavy, rattled and shook, not to mention the leaking hood. But it had tremendous charm and was great fun to drive. Its 2639cc six-cylinder engine was aided of course by a good power to weight ratio. The MG carried the first 'all-enveloping' bodywork for the marque. Just as popular Stateside as here, its 1600cc engine was capable of high levels of tuning. A twin-cam unit was offered which although half the size of a similarly configured Jaguar engine produced the same power. Reliability suffered. Little rust and left-hand drive makes America the likely venue for these two, and the accompanying MG remains.

Above Right: c.1964 Sunbeam Alpine MkIV
The successful sporting Sunbeams of the 1950s were replaced in 1960 by this up-to-the-minute looking creation. Underneath, much was standard Rootes Group fare. During the next eight years, five versions (updates) were produced. The MkIV's 1494cc gave rather less than sparkling performance, and the driver was more likely to be wearing a headscarf than a cloth cap. Out of sight, out of mind behind a corrugated iron shed, the relatively rare detachable hardtop had a better chance of being renovated than the rest of the car.

Below Right: c.1967 Lotus Europa
In true Lotus fashion, the car has a composite or glass fibre body and superb handling characteristics. Unfortunately, with its 78bhp Renault engine, pathetic rearward vision and claustrophobic cockpit, it was not a success. This Welsh resident is probably in the safest place – unless anyone wants to dig a hole.

Above: 1951 Healey Silverstone Replica
Originally a Tickford bodied saloon, these Donald Healey-designed 2.4 litre Riley-engined cars are much sought after today; the original sporting Silverstone versions making a great deal of money at auction. Several distinct body styles were offered, as unique in their way as the AC 2 litre on the facing page. This imperfect replica body needs disposing of, allowing a perfect recreation of a Silverstone to be crafted.

Above: c.1938 Lancia Aprilias
Introduced at the Paris show of 1936, this Italian masterpiece was the last model to be overseen by Vincenzo Lancia himself. Throughout the 1920s and '30s, Lancia had produced cars for the rich, but the Aprilia was a car, if not for the people, then at least for the people's doctor or shopkeeper. With its sliding-pillar front suspension and 1352cc V4 engine it could out manoeuvre more powerful cars along the twisting mountain roads of Italy. A joy to drive, it was perhaps one of the great mass-produced designs of the 1930s. Looking for all the world like a couple of forlorn Volkswagens, this brace of Aprilia's must become at least one beautifully restored example.

Above: c.1953 Bristol 403 Saloon
Another relatively small producer of bespoke cars, The Bristol Aeroplane Company obtained BMW car designs as part of war reparations. The BMW 328 engine design was used in the 1946 400 model, with a typical BMW appearance. By the time the 403 was launched it had the benefit of increased power, and a 'slippery' body, thanks to Bristol's knowledge of wind resistance. After some ten years in the open, this 403 has weathered well. Notice the BMW style 'kidney' radiator grille.

Above Right Page 58: 1935 Wolseley Wasp
Companion to the similar sized Hornet six-cylinder model, the Wasp's four-cylinder engine was lighter and allowed better handling, regrettably with less performance. An ordinary little car, it nevertheless was still a true Wolseley, later cars being badge-engineered Morris. With its rotted roof, and tarpaulin thrown aside, this Wasp must surely have benefited from the watery sun light of an early Spring day.

Above: 1949 AC 2 Litre Saloon
During the 1930s AC had produced some very attractive cars and a six-cylinder 2 litre power unit to push them along. Unlike many other British car producers, they did not rush out a basic pre-war design as quickly as possible after hostilities ceased. In October 1947, they launched the 2 Litre saloon. The styling was different and might be said to be an acquired taste. They were well built and roomy, and with the established power unit, went fast enough. The model was offered up to 1958, although by then AC was making some very sporty alternatives. The telltale wisps of straw show this car to have been recently pushed from a barn.

Left: 1921 Angus-Sanderson
The company had a short life from 1919 to 1927. The 2.3 litre cars were attractive and a good deal better than the firm's finances and production techniques. This example was rescued by Mike Worthington-Williams from a later life of log hauling in a wood yard. He restored the car to its former beauty.

Below Left: 1928 Morris Cowley
The original Cowley and Oxford models had domed radiators, for which reason they were known as the Bullnose Morris. After 1926, a cheaper, more conventional radiator shape was adopted. The car here is known as a 'drophead coupé with dickey seat.' The open boot lid would have had the seat backrest attached. Emerging from its barn, the general condition of the coachwork shows this car not to have shared room with any poultry.

Below Right: 1925 Rover 9/20 tourer
Rover's first product was an 1884 tricycle. The company finally failed in 2005. This model, built between 1924 and 1927, a four-cylinder 1074cc engined car, kept Rover in business until more exciting designs came to fruition. 'Exciting' being a relative word at Rover, whose established reputation was one of quality engineering and durability. Easy for schoolboy enthusiasts to spot, with its distinctive radiator top, this one might well be able to run with a minimum of recommissioning.

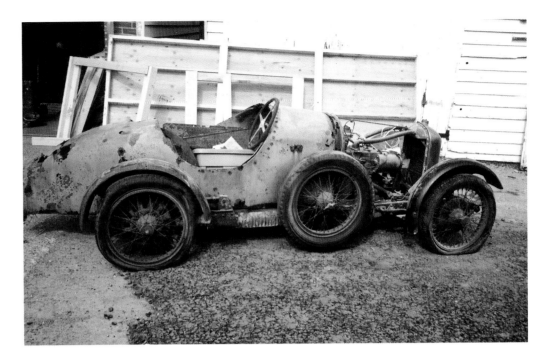

Above: 1927 Amilcar CGS Surbaisse
These pretty and delicate little French cars had the same charm as a Bugatti, although less powerful and therefore a deal slower. They were very popular in England, to the point where many people thought the company to be British. Amilcar lasted, in one form or another until 1939, but models from 1928 onwards were designed for fast touring rather than out-and-out sporting performance. Tin worm has taken a serious toll on the bodywork, but more than enough survives for accurate patterns to be taken for a 'recreated' body.

Above: c.1925 Peugeot

An earlier model than the 201, it was one of the proliferation that contributed to Peugeot's financial dilemmas. Without its hood and only protected by an open shed, it was high time that the car was rescued, when the photograph was taken in 1990.

Right: c.1930 Peugeot 201

Peugeot had been lurching from financial crisis to financial crisis, and the decision was taken to adopt a one-model policy – and this was it. An 1122cc engine of some merit, powered a car that was not as dull as it looked. For instance the rear suspension was made under license from Bugatti. By 1932, matters had improved and the company began to enlarge their range of cars. This cut-up saloon had given some service as a farm tractor, judging by the rear tyres. Now its role is one of picturesque enchantment, fit for any calendar.

Above: 1940 Mercury

The brand appeared a year earlier at the behest of Edsel Ford, who wanted to fill the gap between Lincoln and Ford. Its V8 engine gave 95bhp and its well balanced looks assured good sales. With a mild tweak or two, they could manage 100mph. Judging by the adjacent fire engine's right-hand drive, this car is probably an Antipodean. Enhanced by a fern or two, it could easily draw customers to a garden centre.

Left: c.1938 Peugeot 402B
An example of France's most stylish Art Deco family cars, the Series II is instantly recognizable by their headlamps (missing here), placed behind the radiator grille. The look was adopted across the range from 'family four' to limousine. Beyond redemption, this carriage's last act will be to supply a few parts before being reduced to scrap.

Above: c.1929 Fiat 509
A very popular model for this Italian manufacturer, the 509 was made from 1924 to 1929, some ninety thousand cars being built. A small car of 990cc's, some carried coachwork for Taxi service, which could well have been the case for this relatively large fabric bodied example. Note the cloth tatters at the doors edges. Were this flowery car to be left in the same state in Britain, the body would surely have become compost by now.

Above: c.1938 Packard All Weather Tourer
The V12 engined Packard had long been America's quality automobile, but in 1935 they bought out a relatively cheaper straight-eight engined version; a wise move that saved the company from financial downfall. Many body styles were offered by various coachbuilders, several of which were strikingly handsome, even the factory limousines being well proportioned, if a little bulbous for British tastes. This ex-Maharaja's car, and therefore probably a V12, was photographed in India. It's almost impossible to date within the 1935/39 timeframe. The body could even be by a British coachbuilder. The chrome plated radiator and bonnet louvers were $25 extra.

Above Right Page 64: c.1942 Humber Super Snipe Heavy Utility
Based on the 1939 4 litre Super Snipe car, these heavy duty all purpose versions had four-wheel drive and bulbous wings to take sand or mud tyres. A cross between a Jeep and a luxury saloon, production ceased at the end of the war. However, they were popular in the United Kingdom as a war-surplus purchase by civilians, due to being classed as commercial vehicles and therefore carrying a reduced tax burden. The car may have been photographed in Malta but certainly an island with a British war-time presence. Proof again that old soldiers never die.

Above: 1922 Buick 6
Buick was famous for their smooth running six-cylinder engines, which put the company in the American top-sellers list for the decade. In many ways, no better or worse than the other cars on offer at the time, Buick's advertising and publicity department were a great help to the showroom salesmen. Sporting its Indiana license plate, issued in 1922, the car could well be suffering under the humid heat of a Hoosier summer.

Below Left: 1947 Ford Super de Luxe Convertible
Somewhat similar to the '42 model-year's offering, the later cars had an enhanced V8 engine of 239cid. For another $500 you could have the same car with a wood-trimmed body rather like a Chrysler Town and Country. The Portuguese climate has saved the bodywork, making a restoration possible, although a tree surgeon may be needed.

Below Right: 1941 DeSoto Custom
Hard to identify the exact year, but this brace of four-door cars could well make one good one. The model changed in detail year on year, and for '41 sported a 'vertical teeth' style grille, which became a DeSoto hallmark. The company encouraged customers by offering such luxuries as push-button radios. The early morning mist in Cooma, New South Wales is the cause of the surface rust that is spreading across these American behemoths.

Right: 1935 Humber 12hp
The 12hp was offered in the UK as a four-door saloon or a delightful pillarless two-door saloon, known as the Vogue. Its 1669cc engine gave good performance; the Vogue was part of Humber's move upmarket following their acquisition of Hillman. This Australian example of the 12hp has a local coachbuilt body. Photographed in Victoria, this rare but sad wreck must surely have been destroyed by now.

Above: 1939 Willys Silent Four
Willys were in trouble by 1939, and looking at the distinctive shark-like look to this car, one can see why. Two saloon versions were offered in the U.S, and a tourer was bodied in Australia. The following year J. W. Frazer moved from Chrysler and designs became less aggressive. Willys were thrown a financial lifebelt with the coming of war and the need for the eponymous Jeep. Down under in Melbourne, this car is a bit of a rogue, as the company tourers had four doors, and this has two cut-away doors. Rear of the windscreen, it has the look of a locally-bodied Ford 10 about it.

Left: c.1949 Ford Prefect

Another example of Ford's best looking 'sit-up-and-beg' cars. As with most mainstream manufacturers at this time, Ford branched out with a small range of optional colours. Fawn or pale green was well received as a complement to the traditional 'doom' black. Unlike the other small Fords, the Prefect featured the 'alligator' bonnet that was all the rage either side of the Second World War. If any car could be imbued with the power of thought, then this one is surely thinking "I'm never going to get out of here." Perhaps it's the after market headlamp shields that give it a sentient quality.

Below Left: 1929 Austin 7 Top-Hat Saloon

The first Austin 7, Britain's answer to the Model T Ford, rolled off the production line in 1922, the last in 1939. This mid-run car could be a factory saloon, or possibly it carries a body by Gordon England Coachbuilders. Despite the Austin 7s diminutive size, it remained a family favourite throughout its production. Initially, as it was a wonderful alternative to a motorbike and sidecar; latterly due to its very low purchase price and running costs. As it samples its first fresh air for over thirty years, one has to admire the positive thinking of the 'father and son' team who are about to urge the '7' into life.

Below Right: 1924 Austin 7 Chummy

The Chummy name refers to the body style of a short wheelbase, four-seater, open car. Although Austin's did not have sole right to the name, it has become indelibly associated with the 7hp. This earlier car has the correct scuttle-mounted side/headlamps and three-piece bonnet. Photographed in 2003, and despite looking like a wet dog, this car will certainly be restored, due to its desirability and the abundance of replacement parts being manufactured for it and its sisters.

Above: c.1939 Standard Flying 8

New for the year, the smallest Standard could be yours for £125. Its 1021cc engine would take it to 65mph. Not earth shattering by today's standards, but remember it was only a decade earlier that the family car that could do a mile a minute, was worth boasting about. Compared to earlier models, the more rounded lines of the '39s can easily be seen here.

Above: 1929 Lagonda 2 Litre High-Chassis body
Named by British immigrant Wilbur Gunn, after a stream running through his native town of Springfield Ohio, the very British Lagonda became a worthy rival to Bentley, Alvis and the like. This model appeared in 1926 as the 14/60, the name change, 2 Litre, being adopted for 1928. The later 'Low-Chassis' cars were more sporting and resembled the 'green and bonnet strapped' Bentleys of the vintage years. Here lies the remains of a wood frame and leatherette covered body. This style of steel or aluminium-free bodywork was known as a Weymann body, after the pioneer aviator who invented the flexibly-jointed construction.

Below Left: c.1920s Jowett Chassis
An example of how careful the old car enthusiast has to be when searching out a vehicle. Another summer or two and this chassis would have been completely covered by nature's advance.

Below Right: 1935 Austin 10 Sherborne
The 10hp Austins were named after English towns, such as Sherborne, Lichfield and Cambridge. The original style, a very upright car that looked for all the world like a four-door expanded Austin 7, received a facelift in 1935 and 1937. This example is a mid-life version from 1935. Discovered after this book's name had been chosen, it would seem that this Australian owner has anticipated it by a good few years.

Right: Farm Machinery
In 1998, this semi-derelict Northumberland shed contained a cornucopia of ancient farm tools, machinery, tractor parts and implements. Much would be recognized by a farm worker from fifty years ago, if he were to stumble into this time warp collection of artefacts. Truthfully, the greatest value here lies in the moody photograph rather than the shed's contents.

Above: c.1930 Ford Model A Fordor Saloon
Offered in a variety of eighteen body styles, this was the car that Ford needed to replace the Model T. By 1927, the T was old fashioned and Chevrolet were taking sales from Tin Lizzie. The Model A had a normal mechanical design and controls, unlike the T with its epicyclic gearbox and strange uses for pedals and levers. The A became a roaring success, although it was soon replaced by the first of the V8 engined Fords. One senses that someone has made a stab at securing this car's future, but there's plenty more to do.

Right: 1930 Singer Super 6
The largest and finest of the Singer range, it featured a 1920cc ohv engine. At a glance and with little to use as a scale reference, the large Singer could be mistaken for an American product or even a British Lanchester. Black and white adds to the forlorn quality of this image. Although the car looks about to be put to the hammer of a 1950s car breaker, it was in fact about to go under the hammer of a modern auctioneer.

Above Left: c.1929 Fiat 520

Some 20,000 520s were produced between 1927 and 1929. A smooth 2240cc six-cylinder engine and a styling redolent of American cars made it a popular choice. It was followed by the 521. Photographed in Algeria, during 1996, it is hard to believe that a restorable vintage car could still be found on a scrap heap – but here's the proof.

Below Left: 1930 Austin 7 Gordon England Stadium Sports

As already mentioned, Gordon England were one of the independent coachbuilders who found it possible to sell complete cars, using the rolling chassis built by various manufacturers. This sporty looking model was a descendant of the Gordon England Cup model, which was itself a road-going development of the Brooklands Super Sports – an 80mph baby Austin. Safely out of harms way and usually cocooned under a plastic sheet, this car demands someone's attention.

Right: c.1953 Austin Hereford, c.1960 Rover 80, c.1950 Daimler DH27 Limousine

Two of the farmers' favourites, an Austin Hereford and an Auntie Rover. Both probably at the end of a life, which may well have finished with farm duties. But why is a luxury Daimler Hooper-bodied limousine rusting with them? More at home on Royal or civic duties, these straight-eight limousines were the finest of the fine – except of course for Rolls-Royce.

Below Left: 1936 MG SA

The previous year, Lord Nuffield had sold the MG Car Company to Morris Motors: the racing department was closed down, and the development of a new range of cars was started. The first model to appear was the SA. A four-door saloon, the long bonnet of which covered a Wolseley Super Six engine enlarged to 2288cc. Derided by established MG enthusiasts, the new 'hybrid' was in fact an elegant and sporty machine worthy of the name MG.

Right: 1962 Rover 110

Rover's post-war new design was the P4 Model 75. With all enveloping bodywork, its upright stance and air of dignified grace earned it the sobriquet of 'Auntie'. The range was dropped in 1964, and this car represents that final iteration. Their six-cylinder 2625cc 123bhp engines could manage over 100mph, but one wonders how much of the horsepower was used in fighting wind resistance. Pictured in 1994, the stonework is typical of the North of England. The car looks to have recently left some sort of shelter to be more visible to potential buyers.

Above: 1959 Messerschmitt KR200

A leading participant in the race to sell tiny two-seaters or 'bubble' cars in the 1950s, the Messerschmitt started life in 1953 as the 175cc two stroke engined KR175. The larger engine came along in 1955, as did a foot throttle instead of a twist grip. Reverse was obtained by operating a lever, causing the engine to run in reverse (a two-stroke trick). All four gears were then available for a rapid retreat. Its economy and good weather protection made it a winner. No one seemed put off by its similarity to a crustacean from the depths. Today, these tiny cars are valued far in excess of their performance or size.

Below: c.1953 Hillman Californian

Hillman used the name Minx from 1931 until 1966. The MkIII was offered as a saloon, drophead and two-door fixed head coupé, the latter named 'Californian'. A shade more stylish than the saloon, with its expanse of glass and cleverly shaped rear window, it was one of the best looking family cars of the time. As the advertising of the day said 'Be first with the last word'. This basically sound Isle of Man car seems to have had a rough end of life. Now robbed of much trim it will probably travel no further.

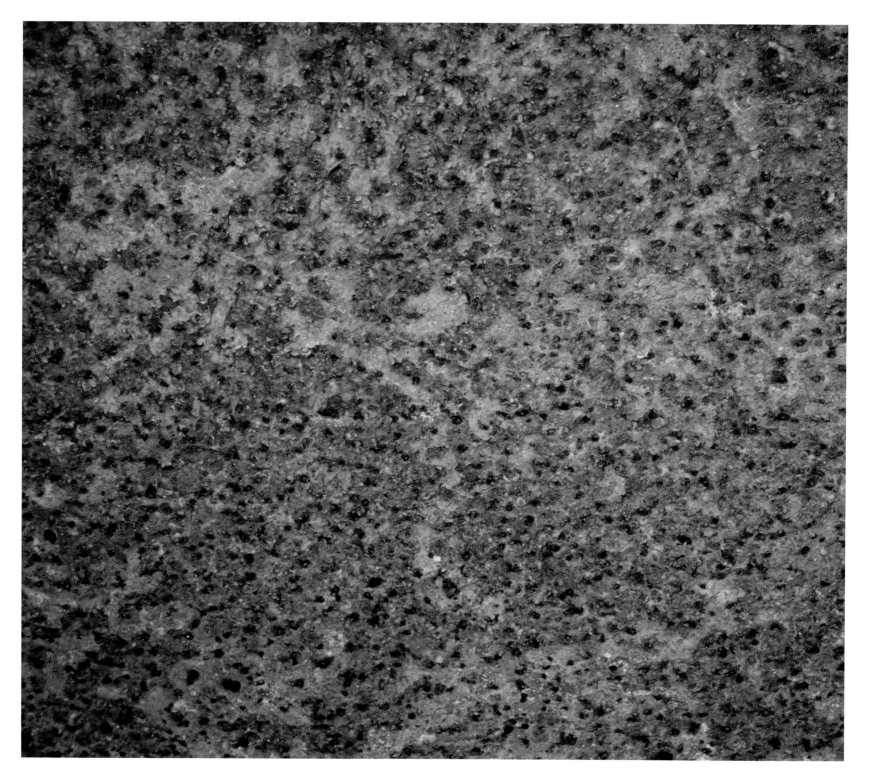

Hedge & Field

Chapter Three

Hedge  & Field

Hedges and fields belong to farmers, and so this is really an extension of 'Down on the Farm'. Some of these photographs are from overseas, but all show cars that have been left to Mother Nature's tendrils. Quite a few were photographed at the point of being rescued due to their age, quality or rarity.

In Great Britain today, with the general public's 'right to roam' it is probable that vandalism will be a problem for cars in these locations, which in many cases rest a long way from the farmers' eyes.

It is interesting to compare the cars in Britain to those in Australia, New Zealand and parts of America, for our climate encourages rust and mildew, whereas they suffer from sun scorched paint, resulting in only a dusting of surface rust – how lucky they are.

Right: 1926 Armstrong Siddeley 18hp MkII
The company was formed in 1919 and the 18hp MkII model featured four-wheel brakes, 2872cc engines, and semi-elliptic rear springs. This Australian find is fitted with the Ascot all-weather tourer body. Note the disc wheels which were a feature of Armstrong, and the trademark radiator shape, which was still recognizable on the swansong Star Sapphire of 1959. Clement weather and being miles from anywhere have kept this old beast alive. It has now been rescued and restored.

Below Left: 1959 Jaguar MkIX
Perhaps better known for their sports cars, Jaguar have built a large saloon model since the mid 1930s. In 1951, the MkVII was introduced, using the same 3.4 litre twin-ohc engine as the XK120 sports car. In 1959, the MkIX was introduced to replace the MkVIII. The last of this line had a 3.8 litre engine, power steering and disc brakes all around. This was the last Jaguar with a separate chassis. RAN 865 may superficially look in fair order, but close examination of the lower edges will reveal rampant rust. If this much can be seen, what lies beneath does not bear thinking about.

Below Right: c.1957 Armstrong Siddeley Sapphire
With a 3435cc six-cylinder engine, and latterly the option of the four speed Hydra-matic gearbox built by Rolls-Royce, this large saloon was in the luxury class. Like Jaguar, it wasn't perceived to be as good as a Bentley, nor as mundane as a Rover. It certainly never achieved the sporting connotation of the big cats, despite being manufactured by a company with lifelong attachments to the aero industry. Car production stopped in 1960, following the company's merger with Bristol Aero-Engines Ltd, to form Bristol-Siddeley Engines Ltd; that company was absorbed by Rolls-Royce Ltd in 1967. Seen here in what may well be its original two-tone paint, this Sapphire shows little evidence of the rust from which these cars could suffer. The doors are held closed by string; implying that the car was towed to this resting place.

Right: c.1955 Lagonda 3 Litre Saloon
The 3 Litre designation was resurrected after World War II. It featured a straight-six twin-ohc engine, designed by W. O. Bentley, as a 2.6 litre unit in 1945. A two and four-door saloon were produced as well as a two-door convertible, one of which was owned by H.R.H. The Duke of Edinburgh. In 1947, the company was merged with Aston Martin, under the ownership of tractor maker David Brown. Head to head with Mother Nature, there can only be one winner, although the Jaguar-like grille is taking a bold stance.

Above: 1954 Rover P4 75
Hard to determine, but this earlier car has a more prominent headlight position and the rear wings and boot lid taper downwards compared to the later cars. Well ensconced in the bushes, the tyres would suggest that this car has been no where else for a long period.

Left: c.1953 Humber Super Snipe, c.1950 Ford V8 Pilot
Humber's first post-war design was in line with most other manufacturers. Large cars, with 4 litre Commer lorry engines, they found favour with well-to-do private owners, company board room transport and chauffeur driven hire concerns. The Ford Pilot was a warmed over pre-war V8-22 model, but with a 3622cc engine. A good looking car of its type, it had some success in international rallying. This pair is ever watchful of the New South Wales horizon and the daily rising of the sun. Australia's wide open spaces mean they could remain there for many years to come.

Above Right: 1924 Hupmobile Model R
Again, an Australian find, but this time an American car. Hupmobile was formed in 1908 by Robert Hupp, after working for Oldsmobile. Like all preceding models the R was a four-cylinder car, and remained little changed during its production, between 1919 and 1925. Although unknown to many, Hupmobile was a popular make in '20s America, its downfall being the depression. The company did stagger on throughout the '30s, finally closing its doors in 1940. As with many stylish cars of the 1920s, this Hup has ended up as a homemade pick-up. Tired and dirty, it was still capable of farm duties when photographed in 1990.

Below Right: 1924 Humber 8/18 Chummy
Formed in 1896, the Humber Company was known for conservative cars with less than exciting performance, but the 8/18 of 1923 had better performance from its 985cc engine. As with the Austin 7, the body style was compact enough to be called a Chummy. Just pushed from its garage, this example has remained in very fair order, and might well be a subject for conservation rather than restoration.

Above: 1930 Dodge 6
By 1923 Dodge had built a million cars, but by 1928 they were placed thirteenth in US sales ratings. The company was sold to Chrysler, under whose banner it remains today. This six-cylinder model was a departure for Dodge as they had always seen themselves as being able to take on the four-cylinder Fords of the time. Although upright, in retrospect, the Model 6 was actually quite a bit more rakish than previous models. Well rooted, this car has been standing for a long time, but despite its only protection being a sheet of iron, it is in remarkably good shape.

Left: c.1952 Lagonda 2.6 Litre Saloon
An example of the car from which the very similar 3 Litre was developed. This earlier model is generally accepted as being less good looking, but with hindsight it does have a stylish elegance. In fact more of these smaller-engined cars were built than the later 3 Litres. Similarly arboreal as the 3 Litre featured earlier in this chapter, this too is but a parts car.

Above: c.1950 Triumph Mayflower

In 1946, Triumph announced a 2 litre four-door saloon with a razor-edge style body made by Mulliners of Birmingham. In 1949, an even smaller version was announced; being a two-door four-seater with the 1.2 litre engine and gearbox from the pre-war Standard 10. They sold quite well, but the truth was that small luxury-saloon styled cars are never a success for their manufacturers. Camouflaged by dappled sunlight, the razor-edge coachwork is easily seen.

Right: c.1949 Simca 6

This car's appellation refers to the engine's 570ccs, not the number of cylinders. Overshadowed by Fiat's similar car, the new-look Simca was in fact on the market a year earlier than the Italian competitor. The engine was a tough little ohv unit, and with its post-war styling, the car was a favourite with the 'essence' starved people of France. Just an engine and shell, this reminder of a forgotten make still languishes in a disused quarry in the Charente region.

Left: 1951 Morris 6

Sister to the Wolseley 6/80, the 1949 Morris 6 was the cheaper car, without the leather and wood trim of the Wolseley. They did share the Morris designed ohv engine, which was one benefit of belonging to the Nuffield group of companies. Axed a mere four years later, only 12,400 had been produced, despite their 'big car' looks. Like many larger cars in old age, this one was probably in fairly good order when quite minor damage made it uneconomical to repair.

Above: c.1952 Austin Counties

Not quite enough shows to confirm this as a Somerset or a Hereford, but the 'flying A' mascot proudly flies somewhat like the ensign on a sinking ship. A moody photograph for all that.

Pages 90 & 91: 1938 Peugeot 502B

No apology for two full page images of one of these stylish and different cars. As mentioned in the previous chapter, the unusual headlamp arrangement can be clearly seen in this photograph. The superb Art Deco styling was executed by Henri Thomas along a theme set by Jean Andreau, for what today might be called a styling exercise. This was the largest of the Series II cars, and instead of looking more cumbersome than the shorter models, its length enhances the aerodynamic looks. Well and truly dumped, this car has survived the attentions of the local youths very well indeed. Perhaps it has only recently been left to the elements.

Below Left: c.1931 Peugeot 201

Predecessor of the previous entry, this model was more upright and square, as befits its year. Over 33,000 model 201s were sold in 1931, built by a workforce of some eight thousand people. Robbed of many parts, this 201 seems to have been modified during its working life. Probably to enable its use to change from admired passenger vehicle to tired commercial workhorse.

Below Right: c.1934 Peugeot 201

Last of the three 201's shown here, this one demonstrates a hint of the advanced styling that the 02 numbered models would show. Possibly a light van, judging by the height of the roofline, this vehicle might well have escaped the crusher owing to its value as a source of parts. A 203 saloon from about 1958, of the same make, hides in the bushes, a model that is still occasionally seen on the roads of France.

Right: c.1934 Panhard

Panhard & Levassor was one of the oldest names in the motor industry, having been established in 1890. Until their demise in 1967, they always produced unusual cars of mechanical interest – for whatever the period. For the 1934 range, Louis Bionier, the chief body engineer came up with a three piece windscreen to avoid the blind spot at the windscreen's edge. These cars went under the name of Panoramique. Several engine sizes were offered for the same chassis and body, but they all had full pressure lubrication and a harmonic crankshaft balancer. This stately matron and the slightly older Citroën behind, are part of the French national war memorial at Oradour-sur-Glane: a village destroyed by fire, following the massacre of the inhabitants on the 10th of June 1944.

Above: c.1934 Peugeot 201

The company had established its one model policy for 1931, but soon reversed it. The first offering was a slightly enhanced 201, the 301. By 1934, the 201 D was launched, sporting a new 1307cc engine of 35bhp. The radiator shell had become bold and definitive, with the lion's head displayed prominently; a motif introduced in 1847 long before the first Peugeot automobile. The car may be enjoying one of its last sun-drenched days, but the lion's head mascot defies the elements.

Left: 1956 Morris Cowley

BMC phased out the Morris 6 in 1953, and replaced it with the Oxford. This Cowley was a utilitarian version with a meager 1200cc engine; not nearly powerful enough for a fairly heavy, medium-sized car. It was not a success, and it was soon dropped, as the equivalent BMC Austin was much more popular. Nothing is stirring deep in this forest – especially this tweed grey Cowley. One pull on a tow rope and it may well disintegrate.

Right: 1939 Alvis 12/70 Tourer

Alvis used numeric designations for some of its models and names for others. The 12/70 of 1937 was derived from the 1934 Firebird. The 12/70 chassis was lighter and more rigid than that of the earlier car, and had its new 63bhp engine placed further forward, which allowed a shorter chassis with no reduction in passenger space. Post-war, the car was re-introduced with minor changes, as a four-door saloon known as the TA14. Mulliners of Birmingham made the bodies, which were both sporting and comfortable.

Below Left: c.1950 MG Y Type

Ready for 1941, the Y Type made its debut in 1947. It had a single carburettor version of the MG TC engine. In this form, the decidedly pre-war looking car was capable of 70mph. However the engine was just as able to be tuned as its sporting kin – and many were. Well finished with comfortable leather seats and much wood trim, these small saloons were very popular. The initial YA was re-designated YB with the introduction of improved brakes and a hypoid rear axle. Just a shell, this rusting hulk has about as much value as the surrounding weeds, but many a passing river craft has moored for the occupants to 'see what's over there'.

Below Right: c.1952 Triumph Mayflower Saloon

Having seen the rear view in an earlier entry, this photograph shows the front of the car to good effect. The style of a strong mix of curves and corners is aptly described as 'semi-razor edge'. The Triumph emblem of an enamelled 'globe' badge is visible. Retaining its brightwork, with a seemingly sound body and unbroken glass, this car must be a candidate for loving care.

Above: c.1966 Austin A110 Westminster MkII
In 1959, BMC cars were restyled by Farina, which gave them an up-to-the-minute look. The largest of the Farina cars was the 2912cc six-cylinder engined Austin A99 and its badge-engineered sisters – the Wolseley 6/99 and the luxury Vanden Plas Princess 3 litre. Two years later, the A110, a more powerful version appeared, the third and final version – the A110 MkII being built from 1964 to 1968. If it were a pretty girl, she could sell chocolate bars. This slightly battered old girl has perhaps given someone their first driving lessons around the family farm, coming to rest where over exuberant use of the controls led to a grinding halt.

Above Left: c.1950 Alvis TA14
As already described, the TA14 was the post-war iteration of the earlier 12/70. The engine was bored out to 1892cc capacity, giving 66bhp. Mulliners continued to supply bodies, and although initially all were four-door saloons, other coachbuilders showed interest, including Graber with a modern drophead coupé. Windswept and with a missing sliding roof, this 14 is well and truly at the mercy of the elements. Ground cover suggests a long residency and therefore a surprising lack of vandalism is apparent.

Left: 1949 Ford Prefect
The Post-war Prefect was, as one might expect, a warmed over version of the 1939 offering. In this case, the front wings became more integrated with the bonnet sides and headlamps were encased. The radiator grille now had a family identity with the larger Ford V8 Pilot. In one version or another, the Prefect was produced from 1938 until 1953. Was this one left to decline for no other reason than it was no longer a fashionable car? It certainly looks as if all deterioration is due to neglect rather than damage. Tractor fans may notice the Standard Fordson cosying up to the Prefect.

Right: 1935 Morris Series II 10/4
By 1935, Morris had established the Series II range, all of which shared the same or similar bodies. All engines were side-valve, and as the name suggests, in this instance, 10hp and four-cylinders. The Series II became the Series III in 1937, cars of that designation being easily identifiable by their 'Easiclean' wheels. Probably the most complete car in this book, as in 1996, it is still doing light farm duties. Judging by the interested chickens, it may well be hauling chicken feed.

Left: c.1931 Austin 20/6 Hearse

The vintage Austin 20 came in four and six-cylinder versions, but by 1931, only the sixes were being produced. The post-vintage cars can be identified by their slimmer radiator shells. Their 3400cc engines dated back to 1927 and were still being produced in 1938. About 50 cars were fitted with Haynes automatic transmissions for the 1935/36 model year. Even today, such a find in this condition might well be re-clothed with an open body of some type. A great shame, as who will keep examples of such an important sector of motoring history; for we all take one ride in the back.

Below Left: 1929 Austin 7 Tourer

The king of the baby cars was undoubtedly the Austin 7. Like a terrier, with its small size and robust heart it lifted the British motoring masses off their feet and motorcycles. The '29 was the last year of the vintage styled cars with the deeper radiator and shell. Headlamps were moved forwards off the scuttle and the fuel tank remained resolutely placed underneath it. Something seems to have fallen on top of this 7, the number plate of which shows it to be in India.

Below Right: 1928 Austin 7 Top-Hat Saloon

One of the body styles offered was a two-door four-seater saloon. It shows very well how the 7 was the first baby car to be built like a large car. It's only with occupants squeezed inside that the true size is revealed. The Top-Hat sobriquet was derived from the extended headroom, evident by the tall side windows. The scuttle-mounted headlamps are where they should be on this draughty example.

Above: 1932 Triumph Super 9

Triumph announced a new model for 1928, The Super 7. As a direct competitor to the Austin 7 and Morris Minor, it was a success, although slightly more expensive. It was designed by Stanley Edge who had been responsible for much of the little Austin's configuration. It featured an 832cc 21bhp engine and hydraulic brakes, the stopping power of which gave it a big advantage over the Austin. By 1932 the company felt it could never win the battle of the small car, and all models moved up in size. The Super 7 became the Super 9; basically the same car but with a 1018cc Coventry Climax engine. It lasted for only two years. Photographed in May 2004, this one is a sad case whose fight against gravity and soft mud is not going well.

Above Left: 1950 Dodge Coronet
Listed new for 1949 was the Coronet range; sedan, club coupé, convertible coupé and wagon; all with a straight-six engine of 230cid. Coronets offered 'Gyromatic Drive' for 1950, which was an intriguing name for an automatic transmission system. Restyled on an annual basis in true American tradition, the Coronet name lived on until 1953. A study in chrome, this weathered example was sound and complete in 2000.

Below Left: 1965 Mercedes 200/230
In 1953, Mercedes launched a new model, of unitary construction, which became known as 'pontoon cars', owing to their rounder, full width bodies. That model was superseded in 1959 by a more angular design with vestigial fins. The model became known as 'fin cars'. The official model designation refers to the engine size, which cannot be substantiated in this photograph. An arty shot shows this fin car to be well ensconced in a scrap metal dump of some kind.

Right: c.1974 Jensen Interceptor MkIII
In September 1966, the Interceptor was created by using the chassis and mechanicals of the previous model – the CV8, and clothing it in a head-turning body by Vignale. Its striking curved rear screen being the talk of the day. The end of the road for the MkIII came in 1976, when the company was sold to American owners. Seen in the Forest of Dean, this damaged and rusty example was hauled away and fully restored. A good example of the old-car enthusiasts' propensity to let the heart rule the wallet.

Above: c.1951 Singer Roadster
The 1946 Singer Roadster was a carry over from the pre-war model, with a 1074cc engine. In 1951 it received the 1497cc engine from the Singer SM1500 Saloon, in which form it ran to the end of production in 1955. This homely little sports tourer is now the most sought after post-war Singer. Open to the elements, the car displays its definitive Singer radiator shell.

Above Right: c.1952 Sunbeam Talbot 90 MkIIA
Another manufacturer under the Rootes Group wing. These medium-sized sporting saloons had great success in International rallying. This experience allowed improvements to be made to handling and engine. The MkIIA came out in 1953, identified by the same MkII horizontal grilles beside the radiator but with the loss of the rear wheel spats. Uncovered in a field, this really is one of those cars that needs saving now, not next year, when condensation and vandalism have taken their toll.

Below Right: c.1955 Sunbeam MkIII
The Talbot name was dropped for the Series III, which was now producing 80bhp. Success in rallying was still assured with drivers such as Stirling Moss and Sheila Van Damm taking the wheel. The model was finally replaced in 1957. The elongated horizontal grilles and oblong 'portholes' identify this as a Series III. It may have finished its days pulling the small trailer around the farm.

Far Right: c.1963 Singer Gazelle MkIII
The Gazelle of 1956 was the first Singer to be designed since the Rootes Group had taken over the company. This later example was just a badge-engineered Hillman Minx – nothing wrong with Hillmans, but in truth Singer was now a lost make. One can only guess at the advancing rust beneath the pile of wet, rotten vegetation beneath the autumn leaves.

Left: 1946 Hillman Minx, 1948 Austin 16

The Minx adopted the 'alligator' style bonnet with a vengeance, which allowed very good access to the engine. The Austin's bonnet opened above the radiator. The Hillman received an interim styling update the next year, which included more enveloping front wings with integrated headlamps. The Austin was dropped in favour of the new look Hampshire. Both cars seem savable, However, the Hillman is probably the better bet as Austin 16s were very prone to terminal rust.

Below: c.1952 Austin FX3 Taxi

Taxis that should have been scrapped when 10 years old in 1939, lumbered through the war and after. The FX3 was Austin's replacement for these venerable Austin 12/4 based relics. Designed to the edicts of the Public Carriage Office, the FX3 used the 2.2 litre petrol engine from the Austin 16. A diesel engine was available from 1956. Still seen in many a period British film, the FX3 was the epitome of the London Black Cab. These forlorn remains are now stored in a dry shed. One must ask the question Why? – with a capital W.

Below Right: 1967 Vanden Plas Princess R

The final and most luxurious of the series based on the Austin A99, the Princess R. The R stood for Rolls-Royce, who supplied the straight-six FB-60 engines (not as so often wrongly thought, the totally different B60). Interestingly, the R-R/BMC joint venture was initially formed to produce a Bentley based on the ADO53 (Princess) body shell. Codenamed Bentley Java, it was stillborn. Apart from the engine, there were subtle styling changes, which even today make it a good looking car. A glimpse of the wood and leather interior can be seen. The sprung front wing gives a clue to the unseen rust that makes this a parts car only.

Above: c.1950 Austin Atlantic

Whilst the Counties Austins were doing very well at home and in the Empire/Commonwealth countries, Austin needed something more appealing to the American market. Initially offered in 1949 as a power-top convertible, a fixed head with a disappearing rear screen was added in 1950. The 'waterfall' bonnet decoration, three headlights and curvaceous styling made a strong statement. Unfortunately, despite gaining some endurance records at The Indianapolis Motor Speedway, the car was not popular. Its size and cost did not compare well with American home market competitors. It was the first recipient of Austin's 2660cc four-cylinder engine that found its way into the Austin Healey sports cars. Note the three piece windscreen, reminiscent of the 1930s French Panhard.

Above Left: c.1969 Triumph Vitesse convertible

The Triumph Herald had a companion car using the same body shell, but fitted with the straight-six 2 litre engine. The car went fast, and was a favourite with those young men whose insurance premiums may not have stood a sports car, and ladies of a sporting nature. Easily identifiable by its twin headlights, it also sported a rev counter. The vegetation looks to be from a warm clime, but where the Vitesse and the companion MGA were sitting in 1969 is not known.

Above Right: c.1970 Austin 1300

The Austin and Morris versions were the 'base' cars, with Riley and Wolseley supplying the higher specifications. There was also an Austin GT edition. These models were extremely successful, despite having a totally different approach to engineering design than any other manufacturer. This engineering layout was carried over to the mildly successful, medium-sized 1800 range, and to the large 3 litre Austin which was a dismal failure.

Below Left Page 106: c.1954 Morris Minor Series II
Designed by Alec Issigonis, the Morris Minor is one of the great British cars. So successful, that even today, some 35 years since production stopped, they are an everyday sight on the roads of Britain. Of unitary construction, the floor pans and structural elements are easily repairable. Theoretically they can be maintained for as long as fossil fuels are around to power them. Once loved enough to be adorned with headlight shades, radio and windscreen peak, this little charmer needs a friend.

Below Right Page 106: 1969 Riley Kestrel
The Issigonis-designed Austin 1100 of 1963 capitalized on the Mini concept of transverse engine, front-wheel drive and hydrolastic suspension. Over two million examples were built up to 1973. One version was a slightly warm, if not hot version marketed as a Riley Kestrel. The 1100cc or later 1300cc engines had twin carburettors, and the interiors featured round dials and much wood trim. Lurking like a lion about to pounce, this Kestrel looks to be far from past it.

Above: c.1971 Triumph 2000 and 2500
Best known for the smaller Triumph Herald, the by-then British Leyland owned company produced a larger car, in competition with sister company, Rover. The MkI appeared in 1963, becoming the MkII in '69. Styled by Michelotti, it had a six-cylinder engine of 2000cc and then 2500cc. Later cars were fitted with fuel injection, but it was very troublesome and soon abandoned. The 2000/2500 were fast, comfortable and stylish, but they fell victim to Leyland's endless reorganization. An ancient roadway is an apt resting place for this group of six Triumphs.

Above Left: c.1960 Jaguar MkIX
Another example of the large Jaguar saloons with the body mounted on a separate chassis. With today's eye, still a classically elegant car, more so than the over-wide MkX that replaced it. As with many cars, the MkIX was a good deal heavier than its forerunner, in this case the MkVII of a decade earlier. Despite being left-hand drive and therefore probably away from our damp shores, the tin worm has been at work; a doubtful survivor today.

Below Left: 1952 Riley RM 2 1/2 Litre Saloon
The last true Riley was offered to the public in 1946, a new design albeit with steel-body panels on an ash frame with a cloth covered roof. Capable of over 90mph, a smaller 1 1/2 litre version was available. In 1953 the RM was replaced by a badge-engineered Wolseley. A tarpaulin is needed to delay decomposition, as the fabric roof was prone to deterioration.

Right: c.1953 Ford Popular
Sister to the Prefect, but with the 8hp engine and side-opening bonnet, this was the cheapest Ford of the day. With its three-speed gearbox and transverse springs, its performance was limited if not pedestrian. The six-volts electrical system and tiny headlamps would have made night driving difficult. Beside an ancient piece of farm machinery, this Pop is gently returning to nature.

Left: 1957 Rover P4 75
The second of the Auntie Rovers, following the Cyclops model, its overall look was continued until 1964. The 75 had a four-cylinder 2.1 litre engine, which is not fast by today's standards. Much of the sluggishness can be blamed on the 'square as a barn door' styling and the weight of the 'super-luxurious fittings'. This one owner car is described as 'looking better than it is'. A salutary lesson for would-be restorers, that even a well looked after car can be ravaged by time.

Above Right: 1957 Rover P4 75
Another 'farmers friend'. This green colour was matched by a light green interior, which did little to reduce the mass of the vehicle. A popular choice, until two-tone paint schemes became available, which suited the shape very well. How long has it been since the luggage rack was full and the family drove away on holiday?

Right: c.1962 Rover P4 95
The least complete of these four cars, and an example of the latest and final version. All that can be added is that it has the two-tone paint scheme and would have had a blue-grey leather interior. Never to retake the road, its last duty is as a storage unit for farm equipment, or perhaps farm rubbish.

Left: 1949 Peugeot 203 Berline, 1951 Peugeot 203 Estate

The stylish 02 model range of pre-war Peugeots was a hard act to follow, but they were very much of their time. For 1948, a new one-model policy was underway, and this somewhat scaled down American looking car was the result. A 1290cc four-cylinder engine, with column shift four-speed gearbox pushed it along well enough. It remained in production until 1960, with very few changes during its life. Icy windows, frosted grass and a low sun enhance this French winter's morning. Snapped in 1994, are they still there, or at least has the Berline retaken the road?

Below: c.1960 Vauxhall Victor F-Type

Before the Victor, the smallest Vauxhall had been the 1501cc engined Wyvern. The Victor was the result of a policy of separating the larger engined cars from the smaller in a definitive way. This MkII was slightly less American in its look, but still one of the most transatlantic designs ever produced in the United Kingdom. The cars were well thought of during their production run, but time told a different story. It must have been hard for Vauxhall to find a steel supply of such poor quality and to design so many rust traps in one car. Bits would literally fall off due to corrosion. There are only a few of these cars left in existence.

Below Right: c.1956 Wolseley 4/44

First seen in 1952, the designer was Gerald Palmer who had executed the Jowett Javelin. Using the old Y Type MG 1200cc engine, the car shared its body with the MG ZA Magnette of a year later. A good looking and well balanced design, they were a cut above the Austins, Fords and Vauxhalls of this world. Perhaps it was a farm worker's old jalopy used until it gave up the ghost.

Above: 1939 Vauxhall J Series 14

Also known as the Fourteen-Six, it followed the unitary construction of the smaller 1937 Vauxhalls. It was good for 70mph and 30mpg. Production stopped in 1940, but continued from 1946-48. The styling influence of 1930s General Motors, the parent company, is evident. A stylish if old fashioned car by American standards, it suited British tastes of the time. No future for this one except to be left in peace.

Left: c.1952 Riley RMs
A brace of Nuffield-designed Rileys, this time both are the smaller engined 1 1/2 litre cars. In the background is a more interesting pre-war Riley from the early 1930s. The model is impossible to guess – but they are all highly desirable. Many more Rileys and this farmer will have a crop, however these have certainly gone to seed.

Below Left: c.1952 Ford Populars
Two more of the ever popular Populars. Even Ford had seen the need for cars that were other than black. As with many mass producers, they offered a fawn and a pale green option, both of which are shown here in faded form.

Below Right: c.1954 Humber Hawks
'You'll feel great at the wheel of the Hawk' said the advert for 1953, and so you might, with styling similar to that which even Rolls-Royce would adopt in 1955 for the Silver Cloud. It was a comfortable car for cost-conscious businessmen and Police forces. The front car has donated its wings and the rear car has wings not worth donating. A good look at the normally hidden area behind the wheel demonstrates what lies beneath many seemingly fit old cars.

Above: c.1947 Morris Series E
Launched in 1939 with its banana-shaped grille and contained headlights, it was quite cutting edge for its day and market. Four and two-door saloons and two-door tourers were offered, until the launch of the Morris Minor in 1948. As pretty a picture as the old car world has to offer, both these cars are past restoration, but what pleasure they may still give to all those who stumble across them.

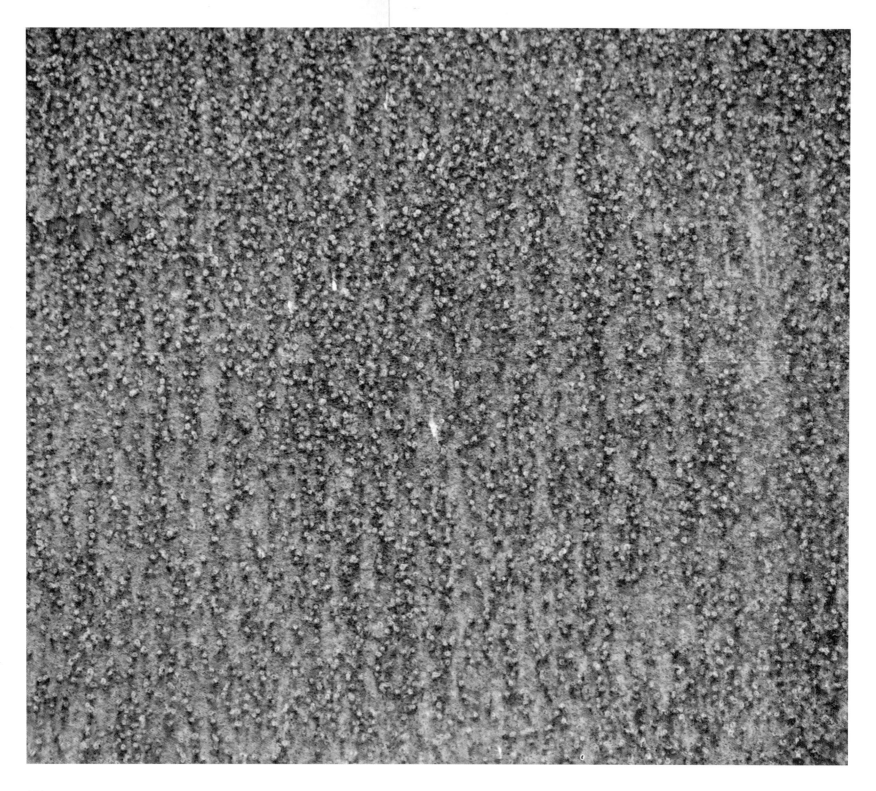

Barn Finds

Chapter Four

Barn  Finds

A large number of these locations are again sighted within the boundaries of farms, but many others are in less agricultural surroundings. The term 'Barn Finds' is used liberally, as the buildings range from timber-framed grandeur to the shabby lean-to with a great deal of lean.

In fact a building with little more than a roof and rudimentary sides can be a beneficial place for an old car to be stored, due to the circulation of air, combined with shelter from the direct force of the weather. A fully enclosed barn, with still, damp air caused by condensation will effect severe corrosion on many of the materials from which a car is made. Add to this the effects of bird droppings, and the chances of a car surviving long-term storage unscathed are minimal.

Mercifully, the same problems hold true for anything stored in such conditions, and the builders of years ago were aware. They designed their barns to circulate air, with the result that cars like the Bullnose Morris opposite have survived in amazingly good order. However well designed a building was, if it has been allowed to fall into disrepair, anything within will suffer badly, if not from damp alone, then from physical damage from falling tiles and beams – several such sad cases are illustrated in the following pages.

Right: 1924 Morris Cowley Bullnose
Discovered in a Cumbrian barn in 1980, the car was originally bought by Viscount Cross. It was last sold to the present owner's father, who drove it across the Alps. This may explain why it's fitted with a Morris Oxford axle with front-wheel brakes. It looks ready for a calendar girl to pose by its side, but the photograph was taken exactly as the car was found.

Left: 1921 GN

The best known of the British light cars which were produced in the post-Great War boom, the GN featured a twin-cylinder air-cooled engine (the cylinders can be seen protruding from the bonnet sides). Although it produced a modest 12bhp, the car's ultra light weight allowed a reasonable performance and a top speed of around 60mph. By the early 1920s the post-war boom was ending and the final nail in the GN coffin was the introduction of Austin's 7hp model – the first small car to be a scaled-down large car. The spindly GN looks as if it's made of nothing more substantial than the household items surrounding it.

Above: c.1925 Amilcar

This French manufacturer survived from 1921 to 1939. Although hard to tell from such a limited view, this is probably a CGS model. Compare this to the car shown in Chapter Two. The distinctive curved shroud of the radiator was a simple way to identify the marque, and the bonnet louvers gave a racy look to the little car. These remains deserve far better than this dark and dank hovel

Right: c.1930 Hotchkiss AM80 6, 1923 Mors S4

Hotchkiss was originally an armaments manufacturer for Bonaparte III, but by 1904 the company was producing automobiles. The four-cylinder AM2 was joined by the six-cylinder 3969cc engined AM80 in 1929. The various body styles were named after French seaside resorts, such as Cabourg and Deauville. The Mors, another French make was attaining very few sales by the time this 2 litre 12/16hp model was produced in 1923. With its pretty V shaped radiator and tapered bonnet, it should have been more appealing. The company was absorbed by Citroën in 1925. Looking Oh-so French, this pair is in fact languishing in a Scottish outbuilding.

Left: 1926 Lagonda 12/24

Now best remembered for the Bentley-chasers of the late '20s and '30s, Lagonda had previously built smaller cars, this being one. Derived from the 11.9hp model, the 12/24 featured a 1421cc engine. It was an alternative for the customer who might have bought a Humber. More Welsh Cob than Arab, its reliability was proven when an example was driven from London to Cape Town, in 1954. Another tired but essentially sound and complete car, this time with an 'all-weather tourer' body. A change of fluids, a cleaned sump, a little air and perhaps she's up and running?

Below Left: 1932 Riley 9 Gamecock

Produced for three years from 1932, this two-seater used the superb 1087cc four-cylinder Riley engine. Not as fast as the smaller, and more cramped, Imp or MPH models, it was still an exciting way to eat up the miles on the country roads of England.

Below Right: 1929 Alvis FD 12/50 prototype

As long ago as 1926, Alvis were pioneering the use of front-wheel drive. By 1928, the company needed a more powerful engine to fully explore the increased handling potential of the front-wheel drive cars. A new 1482cc engine was developed that, when supercharged, gave 75bhp. Front suspension featured four transverse quarter-elliptic springs on each side. The front wheel set-up made the FD an easy model for any school boy to identify.

Right: 1929 Morris Cowley

The Cowley started life as the basic model, the Oxford being more luxurious. By 1929, the names referred to different models, both now with the flat 'tombstone' style radiators. Morris had succeeded by cutting its prices rather than increasing them, and the company was financially sound by the turn of the decade. Offering nothing pretentious on the design and engineering fronts, Morris cars were well made, sound machines. Several body styles were offered of course, this one being a 'folding head saloon'. More commonly known as a cabriolet, its roof folded back, rather like the more recent Citroën 2CV. Emerging from a life of dark solitude, this splendid example leaves its countryside tomb of many years. It is perhaps sound enough to only need a comprehensive re-commissioning.

Left: c.1953 Alfa Romeo 6C 2500

Although Alfa managed to build a few cars throughout the war years, the 6C 2500 launched in 1939 really began proper production in 1946. The last of the true coachbuilt Alfa Romeos, the coupé hardtops were built by Touring, the open cars by Pinin Farina. With its 2443cc dual-overhead-cam straight-six engine, these cars sounded as good as they went, 100mph being easily obtainable. Surrounded by other goodies, this 6C seems to have no engine. Hopefully it lies nearby waiting for a happy reunion.

Right: c.1955 Mercedes Benz 300SLs

In the mid 1950s, these were amongst the most evocative road-racing cars. They were made famous by Stirling Moss and his co-driver Denis Jenkinson, when winning the 1955 Mille Miglia. Production versions were offered in left-hand drive only, due to the cant of the engine. Fuel injection was included and 215bhp was obtainable. More noticeably the fixed head versions featured top-hinged gullwing doors. The 300SL is possibly the only production car that is worth more today in closed form than open. The last roadsters left the production line in 1962. Shaded from the South American sun, these two, one with hardtop, one with hood, are well worth restoring, both financially and historically.

Below: 1947 Healey Westland

Brainchild of Donald Healey, the company built some 64 of these cars between 1946 and 1949. Powered by the Riley twin-ohc four-cylinder engine, the cars were fast, the closed version – the Elliot - being the fastest four-seater saloon in the world, at 110mph. The styling is unmistakable in its bulbous but aerodynamic shape, and as with all Healey cars, the Westland is now much sought after. A duo of Riley radiator shells shares this Westland's home. Frontal damage and an almost certain need for much work on the body's ash frame, make a total rebuild a foregone conclusion.

Below Right: c.1947 Allard K Type

Sydney Allard made cars at his garage business location, confusingly called Adlards Ltd. The K Type was introduced in 1946, one hundred and fifty-one being built. It featured a box section chassis and transverse leaf independent front suspension. Engines were American V8's of Ford origin. Fast and furious when new, these remains, sans engine, could easily regain their formal glory.

Above Left: 1928 Willys-Knight Model 56

Newly introduced, the Model 56, or Standard Six, was a lower priced model for the company. It still featured a sleeve valve engine, which at the cost of a relatively smoky exhaust gave very quiet running. To distinguish the model, there is a narrow-swaged panel on each door at waist level. As with all the company's products, the 56 had its fans, although the model was short-lived. Mother rust has done some work here, and so any rebuild is likely to be as an open tourer, although it may well be sold as the Americans would say 'as a parts car'.

Above Right: 1926 Austin 7hp Chummy

So popular was the Chummy by 1926, production was equal to half of all other British cars under 10hp. Several minor changes were made to the body, which allowed greater width and length (and therefore knee room). Oddly, the headlamps were moved from the scuttle to the front wings for cars produced between October '26 and January '27. It would be 1928 before they found their way back onto the wings. Having faired badly, this car will need a substantial amount of new parts, which are plentifully available 'off the shelf', including recreated body shells.

Left: 1931 Austin 7hp Swallow

William Lyons' Swallow Sidecar Co. produced a stylish body, as a two-door saloon and a two-door tourer. Both versions had minuscule doors, a curved rear and a unique aluminium radiator shell. The saloons had a very limited amount of room, much less than the standard Austin bodies. With their V windscreens, nautical-style air scoops, and two-tone paintwork, the Swallow-bodied cars were very stylish. A good, sound and complete car, this one is surely to be seen on the rally fields of summer.

Above: 1931 Alvis 12/60
This year saw the addition to the Alvis range of the 12/60; essentially a 12/50 with twin carburettor 1645cc engine. Coachwork was a little more up to date on the 12/60, and the rounded tail tourer was known as a 'beetleback'. As with all Alvis models the 12/60 is a driver's car, and a delightful way to experience post-vintage motoring. Imagine stumbling across the car, almost buried beneath the wood worker's supplies, and the owner pleased to see it out of his way for £50!

Left: c.1936 Austin 10hp Lichfield Saloon
Following the lead given by the 7hp Ruby model, in July 1934, the 10hp was re-clothed for 1935 as the Lichfield. It featured the same flat, tapered, chrome and painted radiator shell that was introduced on the Ruby. Four doors and four windows make it a true family car, and it was as popular in its class as all other Austin models were in theirs. Truly describable as buried treasure, surface rust seems to be the main problem.

Above: c.1954 Alvis TC21/100
After the post-war TA14 four-cylinder model, a 3 litre six-cylinder version was introduced as the TA 21. Its final iteration was as the TC21/100, the last figure referring to its available horsepower. It featured a high compression engine, wire wheels and special paint combinations. It was marketed as 'The Grey Lady', which of course led to many being ordered in supporting colours. When stored this unkindly, you can be sure that wood rot aplenty lies beneath the curvaceous coachwork.

Above Right: c.1936 Simca-Fiat 6cv
French Simca started life as an off-shoot of Italian Fiat. Seven body styles were offered for the 6cv, this being a four-door saloon. The Art Deco bonnet louvers gave the little car a rakish edge, and overall it resembled the English Singer. A mass of builders materials has to be moved, but once released this car would make a simple restoration for someone wanting a car that was a smidge unusual.

Right: 1934 MG J2, 1936 MG TA
In the foreground is a J2 model, with its overhead camshaft and vertical dynamo engine, which was prone to oil leaks. Behind, almost buried, is a TA, with its ohv pushrod engine. It was roomier and faster, but did not have the undeserved cachet of the irritating ohc engine. Rural Wales is still a good hunting ground for unrestored cars. This brace of MGs surfaced at the end of 1999.

Above: 1924 Humber 8/18 tourer
This 1896 company produced the 8/18 from 1923. Humber, never known for cars of exhilarating performance did give the 8/18 a little more 'get up and go' than previous models. It pioneered Humber's inlet-over-exhaust-valve engines with its 985cc unit. Almost dainty in appearance, it grew into the 9/20 of 1926. Sheds may well protect when sound, but much damage can be caused by collapse. Luckily this Humber seems unscathed by gravity's efforts, as is the 1924 Zenith motorcycle, on the left.

Left: c.1930 Ford Model A
The Model T Tin Lizzie was laid to rest in 1926, and seven months later the new four-cylinder car arrived. Mechanical systems were now of standard layout, and the car was well received, although Chevrolet were already well established with their version. With the A's new bodywork, and engine giving twice the horsepower of the T, the car even had a song written about it – 'Henry's made a lady out of Lizzie.' On the reverse of this photograph it states 'Model A in collapsed barn.' Perhaps an exploded barn is more accurate.

Above Right: c.1967 Jaguar MkII
These cars may be sought-after, but this one is past the point of no return. It will possibly provide many donor parts to enable another to retake the road. The slim bumper shows it to be a later car which, depending on engine size will make it a 240 or 340 model.

Below Right: c.1965 Sunbeam Tiger
The 'new look' Sunbeam Alpine was brought out for the 1960 season to fill the sports car gap left since the demise of the original Alpine in 1955. The 1960s version had an attractive bodyshell, but mechanics were borrowed from the Sunbeam Rapier, which was in turn really a Hillman Minx in a party frock. Although a direct competitor to the MGB, Rootes were aware that the car could take much more power. With the help of Carol Shelby, an American Ford V8 was shoehorned in, and a very successful muscle car was born. Days away from total collapse, now would be a good time to move the Tiger.

Left. c.1927 Hillman 14hp
The 14 was a popular car which did well against heavy competition such as the Austin 12. Made from 1925 until 1930, some eleven thousand were sold, in various body styles, including a cabriolet/landaulette. The model was discontinued with the rationalization programme when Hillman became part of the Rootes Group. Sometimes the building and the car have just gone too far; this is one such case.

Above Right: 1929 Triumph Super Seven
As previously mentioned, the little Super Seven was a direct competitor to the ubiquitous Austin 7. Despite being more expensive at £149 for the tourer and £187 for the saloon against £135 and £150 for the Austin, some seventeen thousand were built in the five years production run. Another win for Mother Nature, oxygen and water.

Above Far Right: 1930 Morris Oxford
An example of the 'luxury' medium-sized offering from Morris. The Oxford name, used for the first Morris model in 1913 would continue until 1971. Years and years of neglect have made this Oxford look like something in the hold of the Titanic. In truth it has had one owner from new, but if advertised as such, it is doubtful that a prospective buyer would have this in mind.

Below Right: c.1937 Austin 7hp Ruby Saloon
The last iteration of the Austin 7 was quite luxurious compared to its forerunner of some fifteen years earlier. Good weather protection, full instrumentation, a longer, sturdier chassis and better seats, not to mention wind up windows, made the 'super-mini' of its day a fine car. By now the engine had acquired three bearings for the crankshaft, although the 'special' sports car builders of the 1950s would learn to prefer the older two-bearing engines. If years of English weather and total neglect are not enough, vandalism has also to be dealt with.

Below Far Right: c.1962 Morris Minor 1000
Still with its 948cc engine, over one million cars had been produced by 1961. For the 1962 model year the cars lost the glovebox lids and the semaphore indicators were replaced by modern flashing turn indicators. Judging by the rust pattern, this car has suffered from aerial bombardment of the avian variety.

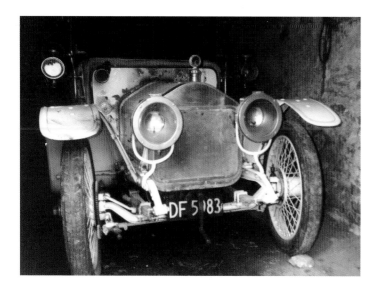

Above Left: c.1913 Wolseley 16/20

One of Britain's oldest car firms, during Edwardian times Wolseley was producing some magnificent cars. By 1914 the annual output was around two thousand units, making Wolseley one of the country's most prolific car makers. The four-cylinder 16/20 was made between 1910 and 1919. The model range was reduced to just three in 1914, this being the smallest offering. The barn shows signs of damp, but the car seems sound enough except for the telltale signs of an under-bonnet fire, around the scuttle. Note the acetylene headlamps and oil sidelamps.

Below Left: c.1913 Wolseley 16/20

Amazingly for such an early and relatively rare car, Mike Worthington-Williams has found another one. Equally sound looking; this one has its oil sidelamps complemented by electric headlamps – probably of a later date. The parallel sided bonnet and square scuttle are again easy to see.

Above: 1935 Lagonda M45 Rapide

The M45 still used the old 4 1/2 litre Lagonda engine that produced 119bhp. A superb looking and handling car, it was a good purchase for those who would have liked a W.O. Bentley – had they still been made. In fact this was the year that the receiver put Lagonda up for sale. The new company then employed Walter Owen Bentley to work his magic on the engine, which resulted in the LG45. This is one car that was sure of a happy and pampered future as it emerges in 1993.

Right: c.1929 Fiat 522?

Fiat, now so famous for small cars, decided to follow the low-priced market from the early 1930s. But prior to that time they also built large six-cylinder cars. This is one such, with an obvious ohv engine. On close inspection a limousine or taxi division can be seen, along with the 1930s American styling. And therein lies the problem of identification, for the look is mid-thirties, but the large cars were pre-1932. A guess will have to be made, and so the car might be a 522.

Above: c.1948 Singer Roadster
As described in the previous chapter, these roadsters were good touring cars, but not really sports cars in the true sense. A young man of the day would want an MG TC, whilst his mother might well drive a Singer Roadster. Photographed in 1992, this car was destined for better things, although the less rare Triumph Spitfire may still reside in its country cabin.

Above Right: 1946 Jaguar 3 1/2 Litre Saloon
The Antipodes continues to provide a steady stream of discoveries, this being one from Melbourne. Stored in a suburban garden, it had spent many years outside with the sunshine roof open. Despite the complete destruction of the interior, and much rust, the engine was still capable of being run.

Middle Right: 1938 MG WA
The WA Saloons and dropheads were similar in style to their Jaguar competitors. A 2.6 litre six-cylinder engine allowed the car to perform well. The most luxurious MG to be made, only three hundred and sixty nine were built. This rare car is seen in Port Elizabeth, South Africa. A very suitable case for restoration, the owner was, understandably, unwilling to sell.

Below Right: c.1946 Jaguar 3 1/2 Litre
Up until 1948, Jaguars were of pre-war design. Offered with 1 1/2, 2 1/2 and 3 1/2 litre engines, they were sports saloons in the true sense, and all for a fraction of the price of a Bentley. Now, retrospectively and wrongly called MkIV Jaguars, they should correctly be known as saloons prefixed by their engine sizes. The number plate shows this car to be a long way from Coventry, but the hot dry weather will have kept the underpinnings in good order; the less said about the two-tone gold paint the better.

Far Right: c.1950 Austin A 90 Atlantic
A rear view this time of a similar car to that shown in Chapter Three. The same use of chrome to make the car appeal to the American market is evident in the five stripes down the boot lid. From the back, the car is not nearly so avant garde; quite acceptable to an English gentleman. With its American license plate, it is probably still in the country for which it was intended.

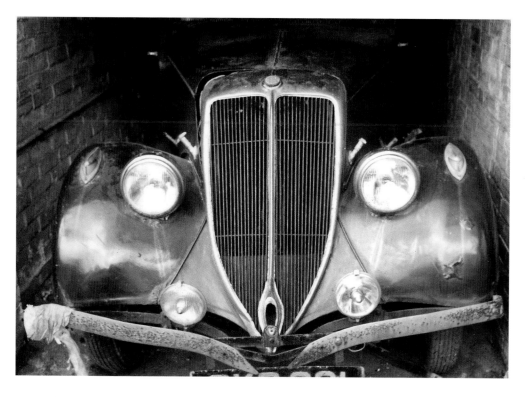

Above: 1947 Sunbeam Talbot 10hp Sports Tourer
In 1935 Talbot fell into the Rootes Group net, and as might be expected a rationalization programme began. At the 1935 Olympia show Rootes announced the Talbot 10, based on the Hillman Minx. By the outbreak of war Talbots were reduced to a mishmash of Hillman and Humber parts, a situation that caused designer Georges Roesch to resign. The 10 reappeared after the war, and was sold as a Sunbeam-Talbot until 1948 when the model was replaced. The addition of driving lamps may indicate that some light rallying or at least spirited night driving has been undertaken in this car.

Above Left: 1936 Jowett Jason Six Light Saloon
Jowetts were inclined to have quite striking frontal appearances, and the Jason is no exception, although from dead ahead, the steep slant of the radiator shell is not visible. As with all Jowetts, the Jason had horizontally opposed pistons, in this case four of them, displacing some 1146cc. Only two hundred and ninety-nine were built (including the less luxurious Jupiter at £8 less) due to public rejection of the sloping radiator shell. Hopefully there is a sunshine roof to allow the driver to leave the car after safe parking in this very narrow garage.

Left: c.1931 Talbot 75
A car importer and maker from 1903, Talbot produced cars at the high end of the medium to luxury market. From 1916 the company benefited from having one of the great automotive engineers of the age, Georges Roesch. In 1926, a small six-cylinder engine was developed that powered the 14/45 model. That car was a success and with a new 2276cc engine, evolved into the Talbot 75 in 1930. Somehow, it seems almost criminal to let such a splendid old car slowly sink into irreparable oblivion. But if rescued at the time of the photograph all might have been well.

Above: 1933 Armstrong Siddeley 17hp
Another make to feature a pointed radiator design was the Armstrong Siddeley. By this year, J.D. Siddeley had made provision for the company to continue after his retirement by negotiating a sale to Tommy Sopwith's Hawker Aircraft Company. This mid-sized Armstrong Siddeley has a pretty, sporting two-door body, which would have allowed good performance from its 2394cc engine. Strangely, for all the engineering prowess and aircraft associations, the make never attained a reputation for performance. Even today an Armstrong Siddeley is unlikely to make good money at auction.

Left: 1938 Packard Straight Eight
For this year Packard increased the wheelbase of the straight-eight-cylinder One Twenty model to 127 inches, and changed the name to the Eight. Strangely, they also introduced a V shaped windscreen, that seems a retrograde step. This cheaper model (than the companion V twelve-cylinder cars) was a huge success, becoming responsible for saving the company after the American Depression. Out of its natural habitat, this car is unusual in being a four light saloon with dummy hood irons; perhaps an Embassy car or a funeral follower when new.

Below: Riley RMC 2 1/2 Litre Roadster
Unlike other brands in the Nuffield group, the post-war Riley was an all new design, albeit retaining the superb pre-war engine. Two open models were offered; the RMC three-seater, from 1948 to 1950 and the RMD four-seater, from 1948 to 1951. Just over five hundred examples of each were produced making them desirable cars with today's enthusiasts. Despite the junk, the rakish lines can be seen, although in truth the design is not well balanced and the less sporting RMD tourer is a much better looking car.

Below: 1933 Morris 10/4 Special Coupé
Built on the same chassis as the saloon shown in Chapter Three, a more sporting fixed head coupé was offered from '33 to '35. The pretty little two-door body was enhanced by the addition of hood irons to give the impression that the car was a convertible. In fact it was a hard top, a clue to which is the partly exposed sunshine roof mechanism. Barn fresh, the Morris sits between the woodpile and the washing, awaiting a trailered trip its new home.

Right: 1921 Cowley Bullnose Cowley
An earlier version of Morris' mainstay in the medium range is this tourer. This and the preceding three photographs show cars that might well be returned to use with a minimum of preparation. By subtly using modern products, paint, upholstery and hoods can be protected from further deterioration, making such vehicles a valuable reference point for originality. Is genuine pre-war air in the tyres really a good selling point?

Right: c.1956 Rochdale GT
A small builder of kit cars, they were the first British concern to offer fibreglass bodies. The most successful of their offerings, this was designed to use Ford E93A chassis and mechanics. In open form, the car was known as the Riviera. Amongst the farming detritus, the eagle-eyed will notice an Austin 7.

Left: c.1955 Rochdale ST
An earlier example from Rochdale, the designers and mould makers had been carried away with enthusiasm for the curvaceous. A similar setting to the last image, but in 1987 this car was photographed in Gurston Down, Wiltshire.

Below: c.1959 Austin Healey Sprite
Long before Kermit became a star, the MkI Sprite had gained the sobriquet of Frogeye. A little gem of a car, it was the last incarnation of small, unadorned, inexpensive true sports cars offered by BMC and its antecedents. The MkI was replaced in May 1961 by a more normal looking design, but one which slowly evolved into a pseudo-sports car encumbered with creature comforts such as wind-up windows and hoods that did not leak. Forlorn is the word that comes to mind, and how much rust lies underneath is the worry that comes to mind.

Below: c.1965 Triumph TR4?
Not enough of this Triumph is visible to make a definite identification of the model. Suffice to say that from the first TR2 in August 1953 until the last TR6 in August 1974, all were true sports cars, latterly with six-cylinder engines. Their direct competition was seen as the MG in its various guises and engine configurations, although the Triumph is perhaps remembered as more of a 'man's' car. If ever a car was pleading for freedom, then this is it. Just a few sheets of corrugated iron and rescue could be made.

Left: c.1950 Rover P4 75
Rover's first all new post-war effort sported a central headlamp, which caused the nickname of Cyclops Rover to be adopted. A full width body and column gear change made it a comfortable six-seater. The expected restrained grandeur of polished wood and fine leather were in abundance, and the inlet-over-exhaust-valve engine from the previous model was continued. Because of the refined and stately progress that these cars made, they were known affectionately as Auntie Rovers. The number plate is not British, and there is sufficient lack of rust to suggest this Auntie lives in warmer climes than her country of birth.

Above: 1936 Rover 16 Sports Saloon
The survival rate of all Rovers is good, largely due to their excellent build quality. This Sixteen sports saloon was rescued from a Monmouthshire barn in 1998, where it had lain undisturbed since 1968. Despite thirty years of complete neglect, the engine turned and the brakes worked.

Right: c.1948 Rover P3
After the war, Rover started production with a revamp of their 1940 line up, namely 10, 12, 14 and 16hp models. In 1948 The P3 range appeared and was very similar in looks but with a new inlet-over-exhaust-valve engine of 1595cc or 2103cc. Independent coil front suspension was also fitted. This may be pushing 'Barn Find' to the limit, as little weather protection is afforded by this flimsy lean-to.

Above: c.1957 Rover 105S

The Aunties were produced in many guises over their fourteen year run. The 105S had a 2639cc six-cylinder engine with overdrive and optional two-tone paintwork. They were good for 100mph. A post-war Riley wing rests on the bonnet of this 105S. The Rover's side lamp is about to part company with the car due to a design fault that allowed wet mud to lodge on the underside of the wing.

Left: c.1936 Rover Fourteen Sports Saloon

With a six-cylinder 1577cc engine, these Rovers were a favourite choice of the well-to-do middle class buyers. A direct family resemblance can be seen with the later P3 model. The single horn and passing lamp are correct. 'Almost running' said the vendor, with a degree of enthusiastic positive thinking that might well have been justified in this case. Note the remains of a similar car to the left of the windscreen pillar.

Above Left page 147: c.1929 Lagonda

Another example of the quintessential British sports car of the late vintage period. An educated guess would be a 2 litre High-Chassis Speed-Model tourer. This was the car that gained the sobriquet 'poor man's Bentley' as it so resembled the other company's 3 litre model – but at around half the price. It is however a lot more than half as much fun to drive. Another miserable lean-to, under which this car has survived exceptionally well.

Below Left page 147: c.1935 Mercedes-Benz 130H

One of the oldest car makers in the world, famous for luxury steeds, outlandish sports cars and unbreakable taxi-cabs. But in the 1930s the company dallied with a people's car to rival Hitler's Volkswagen. Fitted with a rear engine producing a feeble 26bhp, the car took nearly forty seconds to reach its maximum of 56mph. As one might imagine, the car was not a success and few were made. The rarity of this car and its fairly complete and undamaged condition make restoration a probability.

Above Right: 1928 Overland Whippet

The Overland car company had a varied history with a sprinkling of near and actual bankruptcies. One of many early American car makers to be sited in Indiana, it was soon part of the Willys organisation. Before 1921, the company saw itself as a direct competitor to Ford, but realising they could never beat Henry, the Willys/Overland cars were moved upmarket. In 1927 a new smaller car was introduced as the Whippet, the manufacturer's name of Overland being dropped. Of all the Barn Find photographs, this is the least substantial structure of all. However the Whippet has survived with only surface rust, although a good few parts have been liberated.

Above: c.1968 Wolseley 1300

A badge-engineered version of the Austin 1100/1300 model, it was a little more luxurious in trim, and of course sported the Wolseley radiator shell with its illuminated oval badge (here missing its glass insert). Few of these and the other derivatives of the Austin and Morris 1100 models have survived, as they are prone to under body rust around the load bearing sub-frames. Looking good, on closer examination the corrosion around the headlamps and front apron are sure signs of disaster beneath.

Left: 1929 Adler Favorit

The German Adler company built cars for thirty nine years, commencing in 1900. During the two World Wars they produced vehicles for the military. The 1925 Favorit model lasted until 1934. It was powered by a 1943cc four-cylinder engine, and 1929 saw the addition of hydraulic brakes. Car production did not restart after 1945, the rebuilt car factory being used to produce Adler typewriters. On first glance this could be a large Morris, but look closely and you will find the Adler mascot is still there above the unique radiator badge.

Below: 1932 Rover 12/6 Pilot

Rover was in trouble in 1929, their bacon being saved by a change of senior management and a new design team. The first car to be developed under this regime was the 12/6 Pilot, the first of a line of small six-cylinder models that would become the mainstay of Rover production for many years to come. Up to this time, Rovers sported a distinctive radiator surround with a cut-away at the top of the shell. The Pilot showed the first step towards the more streamlined Rover look of the next decade.

Right: 1938 Lancia Aprilia

Another example of Lancia's car for the many, this time showing the styling. As different in its way as was the Citroën Traction-Avant, this Italian model was still seen around the streets well into the 1960s. Today they represent an excellent choice for the car enthusiast without an endless supply of funds. Looking like a Welsh or West Country house, this may well be another 'one family from new' example. Doubtless repainted at some time, a darker colour would suit much better.

Below: 1939 Frazer Nash BMW 327/80

Found in Usk in 1998, the car was originally the property of a King's Lynn resident. It later passed into the hands of the renowned film producer Alexander Korda of London Films fame. Finally, a Birmingham owner emigrated to Germany and left the car behind but unfortunately outside. The engine and gearbox were stored under cover and remained in reasonable condition, however the rest of the vehicle became so corroded that a source of valuable spares was its only use in the future.

Left: 1933 Terraplane
A division of Hudson and Essex cars, the 1932 Terraplane was smaller, lighter and more refined than its sisters. Using a 3164cc engine, the car went well with a very good power to weight ratio. A year later, a V8 was also offered. Hudson had an assembly plant along the Great West road in London, where knocked down kits were put together. The Terraplane was one of the most successful American cars to be sold in England. The single windscreen wiper would indicate that this is indeed a right-hand drive example.

Below Left: 1965 Humber Super Snipe Estate
1963 Humber Super Snipe Estate
Humber models were revised in 1953 and again in 1957, of which these two are examples. Four-cylinder versions continued as the Hawk, six-cylinder as Super Snipe, or with luxury trim, Imperial. Sadly, 1967 saw the end of production for large Humbers with their own identity. No doubt the usual cocktail of farm chemicals and animal waste has added to the corrosion on this pair.

Right: 1938 Packard Super 8 Limousine
This collection belonged to the late Captain V. Twomey. An ex-RAF flyer, he became a Spitfire pilot in 1942, being shot down over Yugoslavia in 1944 and remained a prisoner of war until 1945. His passion for cars started in the 1950s with the acquisition of a 1933 Humber 12. The Packard carries a British-built body by Freestone & Webb. The style is known as 'semi-razor edge'. Also in this shot are three Rolls-Royce, two Bentley, two Morris Minors and an Austin Cambridge car. A small pre-war saloon is not identifiable.

Above Left: 1951 Humber Super Snipe
Several of these early post-war Humbers have already been featured, This is a Super Snipe which was the largest saloon made and powered by the old pre-war 4 litre engine. The limousine Pullmans and Imperials can be identified by their front opening rear doors. The range featured column gear change levers and a mix of old world leather and plastic with metal dashboards. A large Vauxhall, possibly a 25hp and a small Morris Commercial make a classic sandwich of this Humber. Would the registration number DAF 888 be attractive to anyone today?

Above: c.1938 Peugeot 402B Saloons
Coachwork designer, Jean Andreau had conjured some ultra-modern, streamlined bodies for what today would be called 'concept cars'. Although impractical for production, his ideas were adapted by Henri Thomas and the Peugeot body engineering team. The result was the range of cars, illustrated here by a matched pair of the second generation of the 402. Settled in with a few other pre-war French cars, the 402s are given hope for the future by the sun's warming rays.

Left: c.1926 Austin Tourer
Another example of the sturdiest of Austins, an appealing 20hp, or 12hp chassis. Without a suitable reference of scale it is impossible to tell, as the 12 was a scaled down version of the 20. Often thought of as a totally dependable but sluggish car, the 20hp Austin, if fitted with a light body, could give a 3 Litre Bentley a run for its money; although your money would be safest on the Bentley. Nature's tendrils take a timid exploratory look at this old Austin.

Above: 1932 Austin 12/4 Harley
The Austin Twelve was a smaller version of the 20hp. Introduced in 1922, with its four-cylinder 1661cc engine, it was in production in one guise or another until 1935. By 1934 it was decidedly old fashioned, even with the engine enlarged to 1861cc. In this form, the engine soldiered on until 1940, powering the London Taxicab. Owners of Austins were inclined to become emotionally attached to their cars; so perhaps this one has been in 'one farm ownership from new'. If so, it may well have been retired when the Ministry of Transport (MOT) Ten Year Test came into being, which was a necessary evil for old car lovers.

Below: c.1932 Austin 10hp
Slotting neatly between the 7hp and the 12/4, this four-door, four-light four-seater was always popular. Many were still accruing miles well into the 1960s, at a time when fuel was cheap, speed was secondary and a car such as this in pristine condition could be yours for under £20. Note the semaphore arm of the 'trafficator' fitted at the base of the windscreen. Looking bruised and battered, this Austin is hemmed in by artifacts from the horse-drawn age. Note the harness brass and leather on the left.

Left: 1929 Morris Cowley
A good view of the replacement model for the Bullnose Morris seen on the facing page. This time a saloon, but showing the cheaper 'tombstone' radiator that caused so much adverse comment at the time of its introduction. The car comes complete with its original lamps, easily identifiable as late vintage by the wide and proud rims. So often, these stored cars are standing on bald tyres, which shows them to have been off the road at least since the 1960s, when such dangerous boots became illegal.

Below: c.1935 Morris 8hp Series
Morris bought out a new model, the Eight, in 1934 to replace the Minor. A year later it was re-designated as the Series. In October 1937 the Eight Series became the Eight Series II. They can be identified by painted radiator shells and 'Easiclean' wheels. This car is a 'Series' Morris judging by the chrome radiator shell, but fitted with later 'Easiclean' wheels.

Right: c.1925 Morris Bullnose Cowley
Not the most impressive photograph in this book, but it is included for its historic interest, inasmuch as when the photograph was taken in 2002, the car had been locked away for over thirty years. No one was sure what would be revealed. Surprisingly, this tarnished and dusty Morris appears in very good order. Suitably the oil cans and sundry containers on the shelf are from a bygone age.

Below: c.1926 Morris Cowley
Exactly the same chassis as the car above, but with open bodywork. With the sidelamps fixed to the scuttle and the headlamps low down on the dumb irons, this is almost certainly an early car, possibly from the first year the 'tombstones' were produced. Sunlight enhances the cars radiator and lamps, but look to the left of the car and a delightful little Austin 7 Chummy will be seen.

Left: 1933 Humber 16/50 Saloon

The first year of Rootes Group ownership saw Humber suffer from the adoption of cheaper side-valve engines from the Hillman range. Thus the 16/50 received a Hillman engine and was renamed the 16/60 for 1935. Still a very desirable car, this example had been locked away since 1955. Its saloon body features twin side mounts and a sunshine roof. Altogether a fine place to sit on a summer's day in 1933.

Above: 1928 Humber 14/40

A new model for 1927, it featured four-wheel brakes to retard the efforts of its 2016cc engine. Without the front wings, the brakes and suspension design are in clear view, as is the typical Humber radiator of the vintage years. This particular car, discovered in a Devon barn and home to chickens, featured in a fund raising exercise for BBC Television's Blue Peter programme.

Above Right: 1934 Humber Snipe 80

The good news was that a synchromesh gearbox was introduced for the Snipe and Pullman in this year, the bad news was that the traditional Humber radiator was dropped in favour of a sloping design. Some six body styles were offered by Humber, but chassis could be purchased by independent coachbuilders. This car was bodied by Carlton Carriage Ltd of Willesden for the poet, Siegfried Sassoon.

Above: 1936 Humber 12hp Vogue

The 12 introduced in 1933 was the smallest offering in the Humber range, but was no less refined than its larger sisters. It was offered in saloon, drophead and fixed head coupé forms. This example, known as the Vogue, is a fixed head coupé. Reputedly it was designed by H.M. Queen Mary's dress designer Captain Molyneux. Prior to 1935 it sported the traditional radiator and an encased but separate spare wheel mounted on the rear of the trunk. With its pillarless doors and sweeping glass, the above car is still rakish and sold at an affordable price, but the 1935 restyle was not a wise decision. Vintage car enthusiasts will spot the location as being at the base of the Test Hill at Brooklands.

Above Left: 1928 Singer Senior
With an increase in engine size to 1570cc for this year, the old 10hp Singer had been renamed Senior for 1927. Things could be worse but water ingress has hardened the seat leather to the point of needing replacement. The aluminium switchbox, speedometer housing and steering wheel spokes have started to oxidise. But nothing has rotted beyond possible refurbishment

Above: 1933 Alvis Silver Eagle
This Cross & Ellis body interior is in much the same state as the previous car. But imagine the woodwork re-finished, the instrument board in high gloss black with its dials re-faced and re-chromed. Add new leather door cards, and new Wilton carpets for the floor, and other brightwork re-chromed. Then this 2148cc six-cylinder car would be ready to take you on the roads of England in some style – providing of course the rest of the car had received equal loving care and attention.

Left: 1935 Riley Adelphi
Capable of over 70mph from its 12hp engine, the coachwork of the Adelphi was a step away from the highly individual Riley cars of the earlier part of the decade. But the mechanics were pure Riley. This and the adjacent five photographs give an idea of the condition of the interiors of 'Barn Find' cars. Naturally leather and cloth upholstery are prone to disintegration following the effects of damp, and often rodent activity. This Riley however has lasted well. The leather could be re-conditioned, the woodwork re-varnished and the headlining and carpets used as patterns for replacement.

Right: 1936 Austin 12/4

These relatively upright bodied Austins still featured forward opening rear doors, as would the next year's replacement model. Perhaps not the car for arachnophobics! Many years of total neglect have rendered this interior a splendid home for spiders.

Below: 1937 BMW 329/1 Cabriolet

BMW, whose first venture into automobile manufacturing was to build Austin 7hp cars under license, began building their own designs in 1932. By 1937 they had established a reputation for fast and sporty cars, be they open top or saloons. The 329 was a dusted over 319, using the same 1911cc 45bhp (standard) or 55bhp (sports) engine. This example looks as if a thorough clean could return the interior to just usable condition.

Below Right: c.1954 Daimler Conquest Saloon

Daimler started the immediate post-war period supplying its traditional fare of large powerful chassis, suitable for coachbuilt bodies to be fitted by such concerns as Hooper & Co. By 1953 a smaller range of less expensive cars had been established, named Conquest, and suitably priced at £1066. A perfect illustration of the difference between upholstery remaining dry (seatbacks), and that which has become wet (seat tops). The mildew can be removed, but the darkening of the leather will not be reversed, unless a leather dye-paint is used.

Left: 1938 Riley Victor

A swansong, if you will, of the pre-Nuffield Group Rileys. A 12hp, 1 1/2 litre four-cylinder engine and an ordinary synchromesh gearbox did not capture the buying public's imagination in 1937. Later cars were offered with a pre-selector gearbox, but the model was withdrawn less than a year later, at the time of Nuffield's model reorganization. The car even manages to look a little cross, perhaps at its commercial failure or perhaps at sharing a garage with a humble lawnmower.

Below: 1955 Austin A40 Somerset

A Counties Austin, fading gently. It seems fine, but such buildings allow a great deal of corrosion near to the ground. Look carefully and a jack can be seen supporting the offside front of the car; a flat tyre maybe, or possibly a rusted-solid brake drum about to receive attention.

Right: 1934 Wolseley Wasp

The four-cylinder Wolseley Wasp was no worse and no better than most of its competitors, so the best chance for this restoration might be for a person with an emotional attachment to become involved. Occasionally a photograph strikes a chord, and this is such a case. Imagine ambling down a country lane on a summer's day, perhaps striking out across a farm footpath. A derelict building comes into view, demanding investigation. And there is the Wolseley; neglected –yes! Rusty and forlorn – yes! Possibly readied for the scrap man's next visit, but if one could find the farmer and strike a deal……

Below: 1931 Riley Monaco Saloon

Nearly a decade older than the car above, this model with fabric body and 9hp engine was one of the great cars of its day, not least because of the light and powerful engine. So good in fact, that the basic unit was still powering the last true Rileys of the early 1950s. Another car to stumble across on a halcyon summer's day. Brush bush and bramble aside, smell the slight mustiness of the earth-floored barn, and when eyes are accustomed to the gloom, admire the gently fading glory of British car design at its finest.

Above: 1919 Sunbeam 24hp
A six-cylinder model, this and the smaller 12/16 were pre-war
models revived after the armistice, 1919 being the first year of their
re-incarnation. A notable design feature is the very long chassis
dumb irons ahead of the radiator. Only the flat tyres give away this
dusty but remarkably sound example as being a long term resident
of the brick building. A bucket full of money was needed to prise
this car from its Norfolk farmer owner.

162

Above: 1930 Willys-Knight 66B

Willys-Knight would only survive until 1932 as a separate make, thereafter all products being sold as Willys. A strikingly different body style was offered on the 66 chassis for 1929/1930. Named the Plaid-sided roadster, its passenger compartment was painted in an approximation of a Scottish tartan design. Resting next to a Packard Clipper, this Plaid-side would seem to have been painted in a rough copy of Amos Northup's original design. Note the stylish headlamps and three-bar bumper.

Above: c.1926 Lanchester 40hp
Immediately following The Great War, Lanchester built only one model, as did Rolls-Royce. In fact the Lanchester was even more expensive than the Silver Ghost. The production run lasted from 1920 until 1929, 392 cars being built. This car has front-wheel brakes, which first appeared in 1924, along with a detachable cylinder head. Forties were popular with Indian Maharajas and the British Royal family. H.R.H. Princess Elizabeth made her first public appearance in such a car, when she was but six weeks old.

Below: 1925 Standard 11hp Kenilworth Tourer
In 1924, Standard began calling their models by English place names, Kenilworth and Kineton being reserved for four-seater tourers. Front-wheel brakes became available in 1926. The model was relatively successful, but Standard would need a smaller car to make the books balance, which it achieved with the 9hp of 1928. A very well preserved and complete example with correct accoutrements, it probably fared well because of protected but well ventilated garaging at its Devonshire home.

Above Right: 1929 Austin 7 Saloon
Known as the Wydor (wide door) saloon, this Austin was unearthed in 1990 by a good friend of Mike Worthington-Williams. First registered on March 23rd 1929, it had lain undisturbed in this Gloucestershire shed for thirty years. Complete, even down to the carpets, it deserves conservation if any car ever does.

Below Left: 1934 Riley Lynx 9hp Tourer
A shot of the car's interior, seconds after the tarpaulin had been removed. A front view of the car in its barn can be seen on page 167.

Below Right: 1924 Austin 7hp Chummy Tourer
After only two years of production, the Chummy had lost it's 'rope-pull' starter, the intrusive electro-mechanical type replacing the earlier design. The somewhat thin-backed seats were in fact very comfortable, only knee room for the long legged being at a premium. The speedometer and electrical switchbox have been joined by non-standard items on the metal dashboard. Look closely and you will see the brass Austin patents card behind the steering wheel, and the starter mechanism behind the gear lever.

Left: 1938 Lanchester 14hp Roadrider De Luxe
For a decade, Lanchester cars had been badge-engineered variants of Daimler or BSA models, albeit with design input from George Lanchester. The 14hp Roadrider De Luxe was really a Daimler DB18, with a few mechanical differences. Yet another of those delightful photographs where the balance of summer greenery, dilapidated building and glimpsed coachwork, stir the emotions and the heart rate of any red-blooded old-car enthusiast.

Right: 1934 Riley Lynx 9hp Tourer
Bosherton in West Pembrokeshire is the scene for this car's exhumation in 2001. This is no ordinary Lynx, as local garage owner Eddie Stephens of Carmarthen had competed in the 1936 Welsh Rally, driving it over one thousand miles between the 14th and 18th of July. Following the car's rescue, it was displayed, unrestored, mummified rats and all, beside Parry Thomas' 27 Litre Land Speed record holder 'Babs' at the Museum of Speed, Pendine.

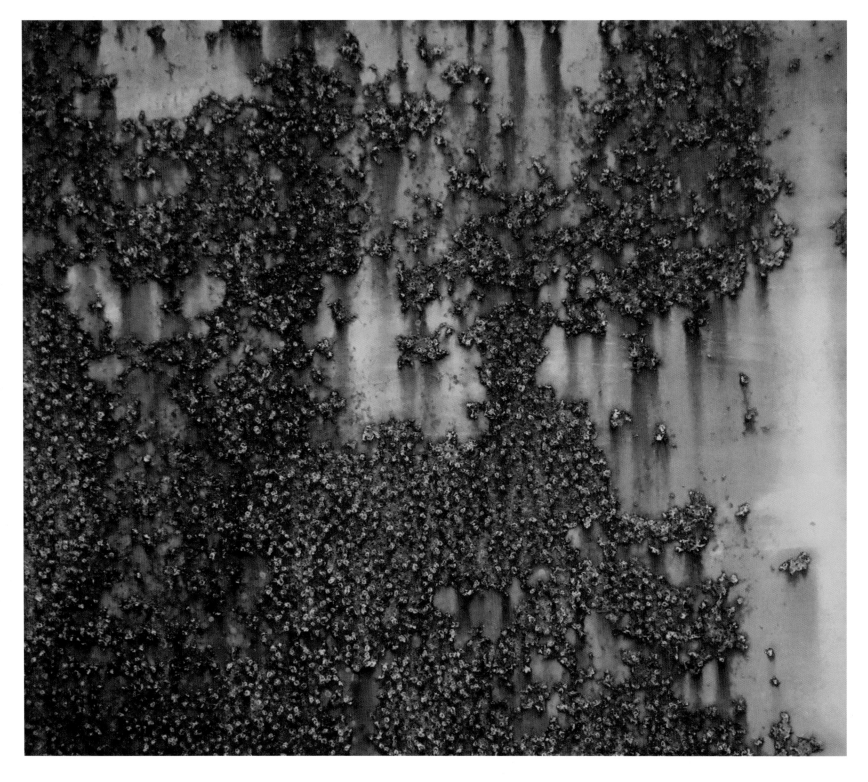

Aristocrats

Chapter Five

Aristocrats

It is surprising how quickly examples of the great marques lost value during the first few years of their lives. But today we see them change hands for tens, sometimes hundreds of thousands of pounds, but when five years old, they were often destined for hire companies or owners with nowhere near enough funds to have the cars serviced properly. Many were broken up, before their time, for the amount of non-ferrous metals used in their construction; bronze, brass and aluminium.

Others, the more fortunate examples were kept on by their original owners, their use changing from transport for the Master and his Lady, to second car, to luggage car and finally hack transport or re-bodying for commercial use about the estate. At some time during this litany of decline, a car may well have been driven into an outbuilding and left.

Another path for the reversal of a car's fortune lay in a succession of less well-off owners accompanied by an increase in usage. This has resulted in very worn-out examples, which now suffer from insalubrious surroundings.

It is almost certain that any of this chapter's cars, if found today would be assured a second lease of life – except perhaps the Bentley in the skip!

Right: 1928 Bentley 4 1/2 Litre, 1930 Rolls-Royce 20/25hp
An ideal duo for the well-to-do motorist of the late vintage years, or maybe a husband and wife owned pair of cars. The Bentley is a standard Vanden Plas-bodied tourer, and as such was expected to be good for a shade over 90mph. The Rolls-Royce catalogue offered a large and a small model between 1922 and 1939, this being one of the smaller cars (all things are relative). It featured a straight six-cylinder engine of 3699cc capacity. The difference between the Bentley and Rolls-Royce was chalk and cheese. Both magnificent examples of engineering excellence, the one giving raucous performance and needing skill and daring to get the best from it – but what a best; the other, no sluggard, but sedately going about the task of transporting its occupants in unmatched comfort and calm.

Left: Garage of superlatives
This uninspiring photograph is included to show the modest surroundings that can contain the very best of motor cars. In fact this is the simple building that housed the Speed Six Bentley in the photograph on the facing page. For the serious searcher of bygone motor cars, it really is a case of leaving no stone unturned.

Right: 1928 Bentley Speed Six
The 6 1/2 Litre Bentley was built between 1926 and 1930. The first of the six-cylinder cars designed by W.O. Bentley, it was offered in a state of higher tune from late 1928. In this form it was known as the Speed Six. Bentley historian Johnnie Green wrote in his book *BENTLEY Fifty Years of the Marque:* "That the Speed Six was W.O.'s favourite among his illustrious machines, can really be understood by anyone who has driven any distance to the accompaniment of the gentle roar and almost turbine-like never ending surge of power from beneath that long slim bonnet."
XV 1430 was originally a saloon by coachbuilder Gurney Nutting, first registered to Bentley Motors.

Above Left: 1928 Bentley Speed Six
Another example of the mighty Bentley, this time discovered in a lock-up garage beneath a central London flyover. Originally bodied by Hooper & Co as a saloon, it became a breakdown truck with crane fitted, and after the war, acquired more sporting coachwork from a Rolls-Royce New Phantom. The Speed Six came in two wheelbases; this would appear to be the longer at 12' 8 1/2".

Below Left: 1928 Bentley 4 1/2 Litre
The first Bentleys were four-cylinder cars of three litres capacity. By 1927 this unit had reached its full potential. A larger power plant was introduced at that year's Le Mans race and it proved itself to be one of the great engines of all time. The 4 1/2 Litre was sold to the general public in standard tune and as Le Mans replicas, in which form it could top 100mph. Found in a shed in Loughton, Essex; like any W.O. Bentley, it was assured of a restoration to 'as new' condition.

Above Right: 1928 Bentley 4 1/2 Litre

An interior shot of the same car, shows the simple but pleasing dashboard, typical of the standard cars. The bucket seat would be very comfortable, but modern drivers would need to be wary of the right-hand gearlever. When used correctly, the sensation is magical, but anything less than perfection in operation would result in loud grinding noises and a need for the car to come to rest before further changes were made. Like many quality cars of the time, the throttle is between the clutch and brake pedals.

Below Right: 1923 Bentley 3 Litre

The first production Bentleys appeared in 1921 as the 3 Litre model. It was produced in three wheelbase lengths, as well as standard and Speed tune. The enamel backing to the 'flying B' radiator badge was in blue for the standard cars and red for the speed models; thus the cars became known as Blue Label or Red Label cars. Depending on the variant and the weight of coachwork fitted, the 3 Litres were capable of seventy to one hundred miles per hour. So interesting is the history of PM 1923, that I include it in Mike Worthington-Williams own words. "A landowner in Shifnal, Shropshire had tried for years to buy a strip of land from a neighbour, thereby gaining access to some of his own fields, but the neighbour steadfastly refused to sell. Upon the neighbour's death, the landowner attended the auction, with the intention of buying the whole property, hiving off the desired access strip and re-marketing the rest. This is what happened, but during the brief period he owned the estate, he instructed his farm foreman to examine all the buildings for anything of value. Nailed up in a barn was the Bentley, originally the property of Stuart de La Rue (of the banknote family and director of Bentley Motors). It had been bought by the parents of the now deceased neighbour, as a consolation for his horrendous injuries sustained in the Great War. He drove the car until unable to continue in 1938, whereupon he locked it away. The barn remained nailed shut until the property sale in 1977, after which the Bentley was sold at Sotheby's Donington auction."

Above: 1928 Rolls-Royce 40/50hp New Phantom
By 1925, the 40/50hp Silver Ghost was outdated, but Royce had a new
engine under development, which when fitted in the Ghost chassis became
the 40/50hp New Phantom. With its Sedanca de Ville (opening roof above
the front seats) body by coachbuilders Hooper & Co, this car was delivered
to Her Grace Constance, Duchess of Westminster. Having suffered a short
period of neglect, the car has now been restored, and is seen about the
various events of the Rolls-Royce Enthusiasts' Club.

Right: 1928 Rolls-Royce New Phantom Landaulette
The big sister to the 20hp during the latter part of the 1920s was the New Phantom. A huge car by any standards, its six-cylinder 7668cc engine supplied plenty of silent power. A very formal, upright body is fitted with coachwork by Barker & Co, featuring a foldable hood for rear seat passengers. This style of bodywork is known as a Landaulette, a term taken from the bygone days of the horse-drawn carriage.
The front wings are from a later date as an attempt to modernise the old-fashioned look of the car.

Above Right: c.1927 Rolls-Royce 20hp
Following the end of the Great War, Rolls-Royce realized that the grand times of the chauffeur-driven car would be curtailed, and so a much smaller owner-driver chassis was produced – the 20hp. The quality was no less than for the larger chassis, but with a 3127cc engine that was less than half the size of the larger Rolls-Royce, performance was curtailed. From their introduction in 1922 until the penultimate year of production in 1928, the 20hp had horizontal radiator shutters – the only British-built Rolls-Royce model to do so. Front-wheel brakes were added in 1925, which allows a rough dating of this Hooper-bodied limousine.

Below Right: 1911 Rolls-Royce 40/50hp Silver Ghost Open Drive Limousine Landaulette
Rolls-Royce made its fame and fortune with this, the 40/50hp, the only model produced between 1907 and 1921. It set standards for silence and reliability that were unequalled by any other make. The six-cylinder 7428cc engine was said to be inaudible. Your chauffeur could start-off in top gear, so powerful was the engine. This car is fitted with coachwork by Barker & Co. Since this 1968 photograph, the car has been restored.

Above: 1893/4 Panhard & Levassor
One of the world's true pioneers of the motor car, Panhard & Levassor were in fact the first manufacturer to enter series production, albeit just thirty-seven cars for 1893 and forty-one cars for 1894. The V twin-cylinder engine of Daimler design was placed in the front of the car where road shocks would be mitigated. When the photograph was taken, the car belonged to the nonagenarian daughter of the original owner.

Above Left: c.1900 Panhard & Levassor
By now, the tiller steering of the earlier cars had been replaced by a steering wheel. Brakes were still external contracting, which apart from being less efficient than the expanding type, were also open to rain and mud. This car seems to have been modified as it was relegated to more commercial than passenger duties, but its completeness would make a restoration relatively easy.

Left: 1900 Opel Lutzmann 4hp
Today part of General Motors, the well-known German car maker Opel started building Lutzmann cars under license in 1897. The cars were not popular and the agreement was ended in 1900, following which Opel negotiated to sell French Darracq cars in Germany. This rare example shows the chain drive from engine to rear wheels.

Right: c.1899 Accumulator Industries 2 1/2hp
The company, based in Woking, Surrey made a few electric cars powered by Lundell motors. For some reason, electric cars in Britain did not enjoy the popularity accorded them in the U.S.A. This company also made an electric coach with a useful range of eighty miles between charges. The front suspension is a work of art.

Above Left: c.1912 Sunbeam 12/16hp
Sunbeam engineer Louis Coatalen designed a new engine for 1912, based on the successful Coupé de l'Auto race version of the previous year. The car was a success and was offered as a family tourer and also in more sporting form with wire wheels and a rakish body. A car in very complete form, even down to the restrictive canvas side curtains with their minuscule celluloid windows.

Left: 1910 Darracq 14/16hp
The French Darracq company was in fact mainly capitalized by British money. In 1906 a factory was opened in Kennington, London to relieve pressure on the French manufacturing sites. Another car with very little missing, a new hood and sympathetic renovation of existing upholstery and paint would make this a splendid benchmark for restorers of less fortunate examples.

Right: 1910 Benz Open Drive Limousine Landaulette Coachwork
The German car maker Karl Benz is credited as having produced the first viable road car powered by an internal combustion engine. By 1910, his cars were large and powerful, easily able to carry formal coachwork such as this example made by Edinburgh coachbuilder Liddle and Johnston. It's not known if the ferns are accidental or the body was commandeered for a hot-house.

Left: 1904 Gladiator
Founded in 1896, this English sounding, but French make always sold very well in the United Kingdom. In fact eighty percent of their sales were in the British Isles. The rear wheels were chain driven through a two-speed gearbox. For a while, the British concessionaire was S.F. Edge, racing driver of the legendary Napier cars. Again, conserve or restore? Only recently does such a dilemma exist, but hopefully more and more cars will be appreciated for their originality.

Right: c.1909 Hotchkiss
An earlier model compared with the examples shown in previous chapters, this one is seen in a strangely suburban setting for such a car. On close inspection, it is more than a little down at heel, but patterns could be taken and where necessary items replaced. The rounded bonnet with sharks-gill louvers is complimented by the distinctive radiator and badge.

Below: c.1905 Cadillac Model F
The side entrance body of this 9-hp single-cylinder Cadillac reveals it as a Model F, the first Cadillac in which rear seat passengers didn't have to climb in through a door in the tail but could enter from the sidewalk, which was bound to be cleaner than the middle of an unmade road. For this touch of luxury, the chassis was extended by a whole two inches. Though the auction catalogue described the condition of this car as "very rough", the wooden body must surely have proved an easy restoration as only the rear doors appear to be missing.

Below: 1909 Renault AX
Louis Renault was the son of a button maker. Thankfully for the car buyers of France, he was more passionate about automobiles than buttons. The first Renaults were offered to the public in 1899, and by the time the AX model was introduced in 1908, the trademark 'coalscuttle' bonnet was well known.
A 1260cc twin-cylinder engine of the company's own manufacture was used, and although the model was intended as a two-seater, over three thousand were bodied as taxis for the streets of Paris.

Above Far Left: c.1956 BMW 502 Saloons

It was not until 1954 that BMW once again had production facilities large enough to produce a completely new car; using the same body as the earlier 501, but now with an all-new V8 engine capable of propelling the car at 110mph. It outsold the rival Mercedes-Benz 300, with sales of over thirteen thousand cars. This atmospheric photograph displays the unhappy pair in an almost mystic scene; however no motor-fairy came to their rescue.

Above Left: 1926 Rolls-Royce 20hp Tourer

A following-driver's eye view of the 'small' Rolls-Royce. This open style of body by coachbuilder Barker & Co was called a 'barrel-sided tourer', for the sides had a distinctive vertical curve. Wisely placed on wooden blocks to relieve stress in the road springs, this car could well have been taken off the road at the outbreak of war.

Below Far Left: 1910 Hispano-Suiza

The renowned engineer Marc Birkigt was the designer of these superb Spanish motor cars; being Swiss was the reason for the second part of the company's name. Although well established as a car of high quality, it was not until after the end of the First World War that Birkigt realized his dream of seriously contesting Rolls-Royce for the title of 'The Best Car in the World.' The other car in the photograph is a Packard which was last used during the Spanish Civil War.

Below Left: 1912 Pic Pic M3 18/24hp

Yes! That really is the name. Piccard, Pictet & Cie was a Swiss company, which prior to The Great War produced cars that were good enough to earn the soubriquet 'The Swiss Rolls-Royce.' Three models were offered at this time, all having engines of four cylinders; the 18/24hp being the medium size, of some 3770cc capacity. The quality of the cars made them suitable for the great Continental coachbuilders to body, but the make is little known today, as few cars have survived.

Right: c.1912 Peugeot 22/30hp

Car production at Peugeot's Lille factory ended in 1914. This pre-war example was commandeered by the Allies for military duty. The photograph was taken in 1998 when the car had remained untouched since rescue after a German shell had burst the front tyre on the Western Front. If restored, the car would be an unusual example of such a formal body on a Peugeot 22/30. The car still carries its military number on the bonnet.

Above Left: 1928 Mercedes-Benz S 36/220
Mercedes-Benz was producing a range of sporting cars around this time, their purpose being to shout the name of Mercedes from the roof tops. Their fame far outweighed their numbers, as although some forty-nine thousand cars left the factory between 1927 and 1933 only two hundred and ninety-seven bore the S legend. Today this car, which had lain under a tarpaulin for twenty years, would be worth a great deal of money.

Below Left: c.1926 Lancia Lambda
One of the great designs of the vintage period (1919-1930) was the Lambda. Vincenzo Lancia had been a racing driver, and coupled with the need for a vehicle that could negotiate the twisting hill roads of Italy, he designed a unique car. A very narrow V4 cylinder engine, a monocoque body shell and sliding-pillar front suspension gave the Lambda its superlative driving qualities. Mostly bodied as almost bathtub-like tourers, some, as here, carried much more formal coachwork. The car is in India, of no interest to the local vintage car club, and due to India's embargo on the export of 'old' cars, it remains neglected.

Right: 1937 Rolls-Royce Phantom III
Sir Henry Royce died in 1933, but the V12 cylinder engine for the Phantom III was by then well under way, the new car being launched in 1935. Compared to the previous model, engine length was down and power was up. The wheelbase was some eight inches shorter, but the passenger compartment was roomier. The car was photographed in the grounds of a large country estate near Aberystwyth, in Wales. Despite the ignominy of being fitted with a Bedford lorry engine, one can imagine the car giving faultless service until the 1956 Suez fuel crisis, and then being driven outside to make way for a much less thirsty replacement; perhaps one of the saddest photographs in this book.

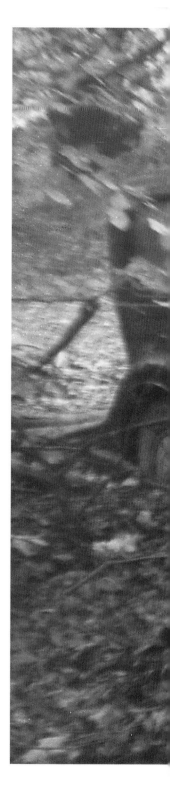

188

Left & Right: c.1936 Bugatti Type 57 Atalante Coupé

No excuse is made for including two photographs of this car. Ettore Bugatti made some of the finest sporting and racing cars of the inter-war years. To many enthusiasts the Type 57 and its derivatives were the pinnacle of the Bugatti sporting cars. From 1934 until 1939/40 the Molsheim factory produced an estimated seven hundred and fifty Type 57s. Its twin-OHC 3.3 litre, straight eight-cylinder engine supplied huge amounts of torque, allowing top gear performance of 10-120mph. As with all things Bugatti, each component was a work of art, the whole being a motor car of extreme beauty. Bugatti racing driver, René Dreyfus, spoke thus of the Type 57; "Vraiment une voiture fantastique." This English-registered Bugatti had just emerged from a twenty year hibernation. Note the 'F' and 'CD' plates on the rear, which give an indication of the car's history.

189

Left: 1934 Hispano-Suiza K6
A fine example from the great era of the Hispano-Suiza. The K6 with its six-cylinder engine was the small sister to the V12-engined J12. Still a large car, the K6 needed all of its 125bhp to make it go as well as it looked. A serious competitor to Rolls-Royce and the best of the American makes, Hispanos were often fitted with the most exotic coachwork of the day. This example was the 1934 Olympia show car, with a typically British body by Freestone & Webb. It's shown here as it was exhumed from a London railway arch tomb, having been taken off the road during the 1956 Suez crisis. Another derelict example was with it!

Below Left: c.1924 Vauxhall 30/98
Certainly not known today for sporting cars, the Vauxhall 30/98 was one of the great British vintage sports cars. A four-cylinder 4234cc engine and advantageous gearing made the car good for over 80mph. Vauxhall and Bentley enthusiasts will argue all day long as to which (30/98 or 4 1/2 Litre) is the better car. The fact that the Vauxhall is in contention at all demonstrates its prowess. In the end it's all a matter of preferred style of performance – finesse or strength!

Below Right: 1949-1971 Austin J40 pedal car
Leonard Lord, chairman of the Austin Motor Company conceived the idea of building children's pedal cars, to provide employment for disabled coal-miners. A specially commissioned factory was set up in Bargoed, South Wales, which produced over thirty-one thousand J40s. Today you will have to pay a four figure sum to purchase one of these single seaters in excellent condition.

Above: 1931 Alvis 12/50
The category of 'Vintage' car terminates on December 31st 1930, and this is just the sort of car that qualifies for the next group; that of 'Post-Vintage Thoroughbred'. Introduced in 1923, the car became very popular as a sporty, touring car. Its appeal lay not only in the purposeful look, but was also due to the relative simplicity of design that enabled high average speeds to be maintained without breakdowns. The last 12/50 left the factory in 1932.

191

Left: 1934 Lagonda M45 Rapide Tourer
When Rolls-Royce bought Bentley, they acquired the services of W.O. Bentley. Never happy at Rolls-Royce, W.O was more than pleased to take up a job offer at Lagonda. His first task was to update the 4 1/2 litre model. When finished, it gained the name M45 Rapide. Similar to the car described in Chapter Four, this M45 is tired and tatty, but with mechanics and the Vanden Plas bodywork restored it will retake the road in some style.

Right: Babs
In 1926, Parry Thomas broke the land speed record on Pendine Sands, South Wales at a speed of 172.331mph. On the 3rd March the following year he returned to improve the record, but something went wrong, possibly a broken drive chain, and the car overturned. Parry Thomas was killed instantly and local people buried the car in the sand where it had come to rest. In 1969 Babs was disinterred and restored by Owen Wyn Owen, who still occasionally runs it at Brooklands.

193

Left: c.1939 Alvis 4.3 Litre
This is the sister car to the Speed 25, with its 3 1/2 litre engine. Alvis managed to endow these cars with huge charisma. A low bonnet, high-mounted headlamps and stylish bodywork, all helped the cars look as powerful as could be. Engines produced 123bhp and the handling was superb. A race across France against a 4 1/4 litre Bentley would be a close run, and which driver had the most fun would probably never be settled. This car shivers in a New England junk yard, still very savable, in this 1965 photograph.

Below: c.1965 Ford Lotus Cortina MkI
Ford unveiled the Cortina in 1963, which became one of their best-selling British cars. Soon afterwards a GT variant was announced along with the Lotus Cortina. The latter had a Ford twin-cam engine, and suspension developed by Lotus. The car produced 105bhp and soon became a favourite in saloon car racing circles. This dilapidated example was reputedly raced by world champion driver, the late Jim Clark. If provenance can be shown and restoration completed, then this is a valuable car indeed.

Right: c.1948 Bentley MkVI Saloon
Rolls-Royce decided that the first post-war cars to be produced in volume would be more acceptable to their customers if they carried a Bentley radiator rather than the Rolls-Royce version. The MkVI Bentley was the result, which was also the first Rolls-Royce built car to be offered complete with factory fitted bodywork. Customers could still have a rolling chassis delivered to the coachbuilder of their choice. !n 1992, this car was surely destined for the crusher. The hydraulic 'grabber' has left its irreversible marks above the drivers door, a sure sign that the final log book entry would have been 'Reduced to scrap'.

Below: Rolls-Royce/Bentley remains
A corner of a Rolls-Royce and Bentley dismantlers shows that these cars have given generously of many serviceable parts. Probably, the earlier cars were taken off the road because of advanced corrosion and the latter cars for reasons of high maintenance costs. There are three generations shown here; Silver Dawn/MkVI, Silver Cloud/S Type, Silver Shadow/T Type.

Left: 1939 SS Jaguar 1 1/2 Litre

A fine example of the last model to bear the SS prefix. The engine was in fact some 1767cc in capacity, and made by Standard of Coventry. Mostly produced as four-door saloons, these much rarer drophead versions are now highly sought after. The post-war cars were also offered with 2 1/2 and 3 1/2 litre engines. The 1 1/2 litres are identifiable by having separate side lamps, the larger engined sisters having theirs faired into the wing tops.

Above: 1937 Delage D6-70

It has been said that "One drives an Alfa, one is driven in a Rolls – and one buys the girlfriend a Delage." Whether or not my great-aunt bought this car or graciously accepted it, I don't know. But it is a splendid example of the motor cars produced by the linked French companies of Delage and Delahaye; albeit in this case fitted with an English body by Coachcraft. Reputedly, although unproven, the actress Margaret Lockwood acquired the car off the 1937 Earls Court show stand. She later sold it into a one-family ownership of many years. It was discovered as seen here by the late Hon. Colin Buckmaster, who arranged for the car's restoration. Sadly he died before the work was completed, and so never drove this beautiful Delage.

Above Right: 1948 HRG

The company lasted from 1936 until 1966, but the cars changed little from the original mid-thirties design. Two engines were offered after the war, 1074cc and 1496cc Singer units. A flirtation with all enveloping bodywork was not really a success, but the traditional cars carved a niche of loyal owners. Two hundred and forty cars were produced by the company before 1956 plus one in 1965, of which an amazing two hundred and twenty five are known to have survived. This is a perfect illustration of what total neglect can do to the interior of a car. The upholstery has become little more than compost and the body's wooden frame will be as strong as Madeira cake.

Right: 1923 Benz 11/40PS

When new, this car was imported into New Zealand, but sadly the owner died a year later. His two brothers drove the car until 1955, when it was taken off the road having covered a mere 8,457 miles. It's the oldest of three known survivors, the other two being owned by the Daimler-Benz museum in Stuttgart, and Daimler-Chrysler of Melbourne.

Above Left: 1974 Rolls-Royce Silver Shadow
The Silver Shadow with its V8 engine of 6750cc and integral body superseded the chassis-built Silver Cloud. Advanced in its time and nowadays admired as the definitive 'three box' (bonnet, cabin, boot) saloon, the mechanical complexity of these cars make them likely to be neglected in later life. Photographed in Bahrain, this Shadow's owner would drive his cars until a fault, minor or major caused a problem. He would then have them towed to this walled garden, never to move again. The Shadow's companions are an 'Aladdin's cave' of the best of European and American automobiles.

Above: c.1938 Rolls-Royce Wraith
Little is known of this shrouded car, except that it was used by British Embassy staff in Cairo at the time of the Suez crisis in 1956. Following the temporary closure of the Embassy, and despite so much anti-British feeling at the time, the abandoned car spent several years in this position without vandalism or theft; a tribute to the Egyptian people's sense of honour.

Below Left: 1936 Bentley 4 1/4 Litre
Rolls-Royce bought Bentley as an identity for a small sporting saloon based on the Rolls-Royce 20/25hp model. Nothing like the thunderous beasts built by the old Bentley Company, the 'Rolls-Bentley' soon became known as 'The silent sports car.' The original 3 1/2 litre engine was increased to 4 1/4 litres in 1936. Throughout the thirties, Racing driver Eddie Hall had may successes on road and track, with specially prepared 'Derby Bentleys'; the prefix relating to the Rolls-Royce factory in Derby. This car with its French Vanvooren body was Eddie Hall's personal transport.

Right: 1957 Rolls-Royce Silver Cloud
Often described as the quintessential Rolls-Royce, the Silver Cloud series was sold from 1955 until 1966. So graceful is the look of the company bodied version, even the latest Rolls-Royce Phantom has been influenced by John Blatchley's design. Why such a car should be reduced to this state is not known, but careful examination of the image will reveal much rust and moss; sure signs of long neglect out of doors. Even small trees are growing through the bumpers. When a rescue was attempted, the hapless Silver Cloud broke its back.

Above: 1933 SS II Two-Door Saloon
Forerunner of Jaguar, SS cars were developed by William Lyons, following his successful coachbuilt bodies for firms such as Morris, Fiat and Standard; not forgetting the round-nose Swallow Austin 7s. In 1931 the Lyons' version of a Standard 16hp, was sold as the SS I. A smaller car based on the Standard Little Nine was the SS II. In truth both cars looked better than they went, but this is more a compliment to their coachwork than a slur on their mechanics. Dry and undamaged, with wings at the back of the shed, this car should be an easy and rewarding restoration.

Above Left: 1937 SS 100
By now the SS cars had grown into sports cars of beauty, the 100 having an engine of 2 1/2 litres and a putative speed of 100mph. When the car was sixteen months old, the second owner took delivery, using it as an everyday car until 1965. It was kept by him and then his widow up until 1994. It survived rallying in the 1930s, being barn-stored for the duration of the Second World War and suffering mild damage during the 1987 Hurricane. In 1994, the car was sold at auction, in this condition for £55,000 plus commission.

Left: 1937 SS 100
I make no apology for including this posed 'auction catalogue' photograph of the car above. It says so much of what the rescuing of old cars is all about. Yes! A restorer must have a good deal of money, but if his or her heart is not stirred by the potential purchase, then the car will never be enjoyed – walk away.

Right: 1961 Jaguar E Type
9600 HP was the fifth production E Type and was used for the model's press launch in Geneva. The motoring world had seen nothing like the E type, and today it remains one of the most sensuous sports cars ever built. Originally powered by the XK twin overhead camshaft engine, and from 1971 by the Jaguar V12 cylinder unit, the E type slowly gained weight and lost its pure looks to the gods of American and European safety legislation. Here, 9600 HP sits in its home of many years, unrecognized for what an historic car it is. The photograph looks posed, but in truth only the careful placing of the camera has been used to enhance the car's surroundings. Today, 9600 HP is fully restored and on the road.

Commercially Speaking

Chapter Six

Commercially Speaking

Commercials, lorries, trucks, vans, coaches and buses, call them what you will, are large and unloved. They are a means to an end, a device to help their owners in their business endeavours. When they are no longer commercially viable they are usually cut up for scrap.

They do have chances of survival that are not available to smaller vehicles; their use as a storage facility, office or living accommodation. The location for the appearance of Dr. Who's Tardis in the first episode of the iconic television series was in a small scrap-yard in the London Borough of Acton. In real life the yard's 'office' was an old double-decker bus. In country areas, an old pantechnicon makes a cheap and immediate small barn, and an old lorry chassis, a good basis for a shepherd's hut. More than one family has lived a happy life in a converted coach, unacceptable in the new millennium, but fifty years ago things were different.

Judging by the following photographs, I suspect my sentiment expressed in the first paragraph is not totally true. More than one of these work horses has been allowed to slumber in a corner of a yard or field; perhaps it was the company's first vehicle, or the one that earnt the most money, or the last of a favourite model. Whatever the reason, not a few of their hard-headed businessmen owners, despite their gruff exteriors, had a soft spot for the 'old girls'.

Right: c.1980 Leyland Terrier
Islands continue to provide a rich source of discoveries, because it is too expensive to export the scrap vehicle when it reaches the end of its life. This Leyland Terrier, 'out to grass' in Cyprus is typical. You can bet that it had a hard life before abandonment.

204

Above c.1958 Fiat
This example was assembled in Fiat's Yugoslavian plant. Dumped or broken down, it will not have lasted long on the edge of the public highway. The next stop will surely be at the scrap-yard.

Above Left: 1949 Austin K8 Three Way
Austin, better known for car production, had produced commercial vehicles since before the First World War. In the late 1940s and early '50s, the 25cwt K8 was a popular delivery and general purpose lorry. The 'Three Way' name refers to the fact that the usual rear doors were supplemented by narrow double doors on each side.

Left: c.1955 Ford Thames
Pre-war Ford commercial vehicles had been sold under the name of Fordson. From 1939 onwards the appellation Ford came into use. The Thames came as a 2 ton or 3 ton chassis, with 4-cylinder petrol or diesel engines. The latter had the cleverly-designed radiator badge '4D'.

Above: c.1925 Dodge Four
Another converted car chassis, this one was probably used as a tender to take water to animals on a New Zealand cattle station. Note the strange chain driven shaft to the right of the radiator; a pumping mechanism perhaps.

Right: c.1960 Ford Thames Trader
The model in the photograph on the facing page, below left was replaced in 1957 by the Thames Trader. Easily recognizable by its 'droop snoot' and 'stubby' cooling vent, this cab style was used across the Ford range for 2 to 8-ton chassis'.

Left: Chevrolet, Bedford, Ford, Morris Commercial, International, Fordson
Judging by the blue skies, right-hand steering and mix of British and American makes, this is an Australian or New Zealand setting. Illustrating features from the 1940s and '50s, the work of the design stylists has clearly been influenced by the car divisions of each company.

Right: c.1930 Renault
The farmers of France have a reputation for frugality, second to none. This, coupled with the wartime occupation meant that vehicles remained in use far longer than their makers intended. The late John Bolster encapsulated the situation of French country cars thus: "in that state of utter neglect that only the French are capable." This Renault started out as a car, possibly a Vivasix model, but when passenger duties were done, it became a pick up truck.

Above Left: c.1954 Albion
Civilian models were reintroduced in 1947, of which this is probably a
1 1/2 ton AZ5 model. Note the traditional wood frame and aluminium
panelled construction of the cab, a method that only the best of car
coachbuilders were still using at the time.

Below Left: c.1947 Albion
An eight-wheeler, with four-wheel steering, this is an example of dereliction
suffered at the hands of Lyon's Yard. If the owner had sold vehicles when
requested, then restoration tasks as large as this could have been
avoided. So, once again the breakers torch was the likely end to this
Albion's life.

Right: c.1936 Albion
Albion of Bathgate in Scotland used the slogan 'Sure as the Sunrise',
to reflect the distinctive top to their radiators. This example was
photographed in 1999, shortly before Lyon's Yard was cleared for
redevelopment. Sporting its history on the door, this hard worked
example would be a mammoth restoration task.

Above Left: c.1942 Bedford OY
Vauxhall Motors' truck division, Bedford was one of the first companies to begin Second World War military vehicle production in earnest. The OY model was built to British government specifications. Capable of carrying 3 tons, and powered by a 72hp six-cylinder engine, it became a mainstay of British forces throughout all theatres of the war.

Below Left: 1942 Bedford OY
Pictured in 1998, when the son of the original owner of this civilian-allocated Bedford discovered the lorry less than a mile from his home. A 1939 long wheelbase Bedford had been commandeered by the Army in 1939, and three years later, this was the replacement. From 1944 to 1958, it ran three or four times a week, fully laden both ways, on the London to Birmingham route. Sold in 1960, its history in the intervening years is unknown. Restoration has been completed.

Right: 1960 Ford Thames
Another example of a Ford Thames, only this one has been a long-time resident of a field. Way beyond repair, it still has a few worthy parts to keep a sister or two on the road.

Above: 1948 Morris Commercial LC4
Photographed in Sydney, this 1 1/2 ton pick up is fitted with the optional
Saurer-built diesel engine. Although a forward-control model was also
offered, this good-looking design remained a favourite. Look closely and
you can see that the cab is serving duty as a splendid hothouse.

Right: c.1949 Morris Commercial One Ton Van
Morris' post-war offering until the LD range
came out in 1952. This earlier version is best
remembered as Metropolitan Police 'Black
Marias' used for transporting prisoners.

Below: 1949 Morris Commercial FV Series I
An example of the forward control 5-ton chassis, which by placing the cab directly over the engine allowed a greater volume of payload to be carried. Note the rear hinged doors, a particularly pre-war feature. The family resemblance to the lorry in the lower photograph can be seen in the design of the radiator grille.

Above Right: 1958 Morris Commercial LC5
By this time, the same basic vehicle as the pre-war LC3 had evolved, the most visible feature being the faired in lights. Although the LC5 was only offered as a 2 1/2 ton payload vehicle, this one has twin rear wheels.

Above: c.1930 Morris Commercial L2
Morris started building true commercial vehicles in 1924. First offering was a 1 ton chassis, but from 1930 onwards a range of 8cwt, 10cwt and 12cwt variants appeared. This one was found in Salisbury, and carries many of the mechanical parts of a similar L2 model. Restoration was undertaken in Haverfordwest.

Above: 1922 Leyland

The model is unknown, but the halves of this Australian delivered chassis are reunited after suffering the fate of many large cars and trucks in the 'sunburnt country'; that of being cut up, the front to become a power source to drive machinery or pump water and the rear to become a trailer.

Above Left: c.1916 Fiat Lorry

A rare sight today, but not a few worn out commercial vehicles ended their days as foundations for living accommodation of some type or another. Mobile workshops, shepherds' huts and 'home sweet home', were but a few of their uses. In civilian life this was home for a gang of itinerant wood cutters. Their saw bench was driven from a jacked-up rear wheel. It was abandoned in Mid Wales and now serves as a winter-feed store for sheep.

Left: c.1925 Republic

An Australian discovery in 1994, alongside a pair of World War II Jeeps, was this American truck. Founded in 1913 as the Alma Motor Truck Company of Alma Michigan, the name was changed the following year to Republic. The company merged with fire engine makers American La France in 1929, although truck production continued under the name Republic until 1931. A quick glance would suggest Daimler, with the fluted radiator top, but the manufacturers name is cast deeply into the component. Note the acetylene gas headlamps.

Right: c.1918 International Model G

The American International Harvester Corporation was formed in 1902, to manufacture farming equipment. They soon branched out into commercial vehicles, starting with their 'horse and buggy' style 'High Wheeler' trucks. This more modern offering looks much like a Renault, with its 'coal scuttle' bonnet. Not so abundant as the wartime Mack trucks, the 4-cylinder, Model G, 2 ton International did its bit for the war effort.

Below Left: c.1955 Bedford S Type Fire Engine
The first all new post-war Bedford, was the S type. Although an immensely popular civilian vehicle, it is well known as the archetype 'army lorry' of its day. Its most famous role has been, indeed still is, as the 'Green Goddess' fire engine. Originally designed to act as wayside water pumping units in the case of nuclear war, they have for over fifty years acted as reserve fire engines, in times of national emergency and strikes. The engines pictured here appear to be red in colour, and therefore not true 'Green Goddesses.'

Right: Chevrolet CMP
Canadian built to British specifications, many thousands of the CMP (Canadian Military Pattern) vehicles were produced during World War II by Chevrolet and Ford: capacities ranged from 8cwt to 8 tons. At war's end many, some even unused, were sold into the civilian market. The strange looking downward slanting windscreen was designed to avoid reflecting sunlight into the eagle eyes of enemy reconnaissance pilots during the North Africa campaign.

Above: c.1953 Humber FV1601
Humber had supplied staff cars during the war, some armoured and some for desert duty. Field Marshall Lord Montgomery placed great trust in his Snipe tourer 'Old Faithful' during the Africa campaign. These one ton trucks were a post-war offering, fitted with Rolls-Royce B60 engines. Despite offering variable-height independent suspension, soft-skin or armoured bodies for a variety of roles, they were not hugely successful.

Below: c.1943 Austin K2 Ambulance
Very similar in cab design to the Bedford product of the same era, the Series K Austin was offered in versions from 30cwt to 5 tons. New for 1938, the Series K was supplied in many guises during the war. Their similarity to the Bedford earned them the sobriquet of 'Birmingham Bedfords'.

Above: c.1947 Bedford O Series
Having suffered the ignominy of dereliction and partial burial, this flatbed is seeing out its days as a hothouse for brambles and weeds. The location is most probably in Britain, as the British Rail coach and three-wheel Reliant Robin will testify.

Left: c.1960 Bedford Cab
At a time when smaller commercial models were offered as normal control (engine in front) or forward control (cab over engine), this Bedford shows the American parentage of its parent company General Motors. Due to its size, simplicity and transatlantic looks, these Bedfords are often seen at commercial vehicle rallies.

Above Right: c.1949 Bedford K,M or O Series
The Bedford K, M and O Series were launched in 1938, being adapted for military use throughout the war. Re-introduced to the civilian market in 1946, they continued until 1953. The letter designations ran thus: K, 30-40cwt, M, 2-3 tons and O, 4-5 tons. The range was as popular abroad as it was in the home market, as they were adapted to just about every use one can imagine.

Right: 1949 Bedford O Series
Taken out of service in 1969, by owners B. I. Hope and Sons of Burbage, near Marlborough, this lorry was photographed in 2001. The new owner intended to restore the vehicle to be used as transportation for his motorcycle collection. The original registration number has been recovered.

Above Right: c.1952 Scammell Pioneer
A different view of a different Scammell, this time identified as a Pioneer. A wartime model used for tank and heavy gun transport, many found favour with travelling fairgrounds, when sold off as war surplus.

Below Right: c.1947 Bedford M Series
Many years have passed since the Brookside garage towed in a breakdown with this Bedford. Although the alternative of a Perkins diesel engine was offered for the model, the six easily visible sparking plugs show this to be a petrol fuelled example. Note that the winch would have been hand-operated without the aid of electric motors or hydraulics.

Left: Scammell Recovery Tractor
Scammell is a name long associated with the heaviest of British-built haulage tractor units. A company with a long and illustrious history, it had the misfortune to be absorbed into the Leyland Empire which ensured its demise along with the major part of British commercial vehicle manufacture. This early post-war example still carries the 'coffee-pot' radiator cap that was a steam condenser.

Above Left: 1953 Fordson E83W Van
Known less formally as the 10cwt van, the E83W was introduced in 1938 and remained in production until 1957. With its 1172cc engine, three-speed gearbox, transverse springing and 6-volt electrical system it was basic to say the least. The strange model designation referred to 'E' for England, '8' for 1938 introduction, '3' for 10hp, 'W' for commercial.

Below Far Left: 1953 Fordson E83W
Same model, different field. Corrosion is not so far advanced, but the same weaknesses are apparent. The front quarter of another Bedford O series has just made its way into the photograph.

Below Left: c.1953 Standard Vanguard Pick-up
Based on the all new post-war car of 1946, van and pick-up versions were also offered. Although a few companies in the United Kingdom used them, sales were most successful abroad. Survivors are rare, and this one seen in Crete during 1991 seems to have survived a hard life fairly well.

Above Right: c.1924 Austin 7hp
Throughout the life of the much-loved Austin 7, a van version was offered. With a capacity of only 2 1/2cwt, it was very much a light delivery vehicle or transport for travelling salesmen. The early vans, based on the Chummy, featured C shaped cut-aways above the waist high doors. This example is not correct, and would suggest a replica body similar to the original.

Below Right: c.1953 Austin 10cwt Van
Just like the Standard Vanguard van and pick-up, the Austin versions were good sellers abroad. Based on the four-door Devon and two-door Dorset saloons, the 10cwt continued to be built after the passenger vehicles' demise in 1952. In fact they lasted until 1955, when the Austin Cambridge based commercials took over.

Above Left: c.1928 International 10/20, c.1924 Hart-Parr
Pictured in Queensland, the International is to the rear. Produced from 1922 – 1939, it was the best known of the International Group's tractors of the period. The Hart-Parr, a competitor, featured a twin-cylinder horizontally opposed engine.

Below Left: c.1925-35 Tractors
Again, sighted in Queensland, Australia, this row of eight tractors are possibly examples of, from the left, a pair of Massey Harris or Wallis, Fordson E27N, Fordson Standard, Lanz Bulldog, unknown, unknown, Lanz Bulldog.

Above Right: c.1936 Fordson Standard Tractor
Only ten years ago, vehicles like this could be found in rural scrap-yards, but that was before European legislation forced their closure. Spotted in Lampeter, South Wales, this model was developed in America in 1917. It sold in the U.K. until 1946, with very few modifications.

Below Right: c.1960 Nuffield 4/60
This British-built tractor, fitted with a BMC diesel engine after their takeover of the Nuffield Group, was later sold as a Leyland. This necessitated a change of tinwork and paint; but beneath, it was essentially the same tractor.

Below Far Right: 1938 McCormick-Deering W-30
International Harvester produced tractors under their own name, McCormick-Deering and Farmall. This was a standard-tread version of the Farmall F-30 row crop tractor. Built from 1932 until 1940, it was a general-purpose tractor and sold well at home and abroad. At $975 it undersold many competitors, making the bright red W-30s a common sight.

Left: c1960 Dennis
At the end of their working lives, buses and coaches often end up in remote places, being used as living accommodation or for storage. This one however has its seats intact and would therefore have been abandoned. Seen in the Scottish Highlands, it has been robbed of all its aluminium outer panelling – presumably for its scrap metal value..

Above Right: c.1939 Dennis Bus
An earlier Dennis than the previous example, this would also be a serious restoration project, although the joint efforts of the members of a bus preservation group would spread the workload and financial burden. Dennis is best known for their fire engines, but transport vehicles for people and goods were also built.

Below Right: c.1949 AEC Coach, c.1949 Bristol Bus
Both these wrecks illustrate the 'half-cab' design, where the driver's cab is separated from the main passenger compartment, and has the engine alongside. The AEC, would have been manufactured in Southall, where the majority of London buses were built, and the Bristol came from the factory situated in the city from which it took its name. Note the large route-destination box atop the Bristol bus, compared to the small 'window' that would have housed the coach operator's name.

Back To Nature

Chapter Seven

Back To Nature

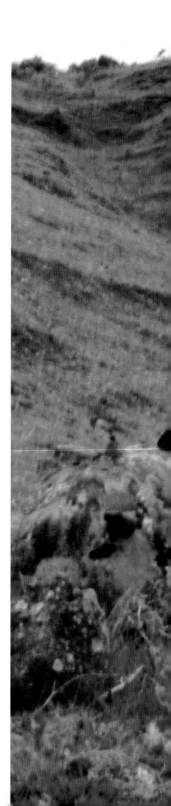

This chapter illustrates vehicles which were kept for a generally unfathomable reason. The scrap-yard cars were retained as they had a perceived value to the business, but the ones abandoned in fields, woods and gardens are more of a mystery. Most likely their owners had an emotional attachment to them, which gave their rose-coloured spectacles a very deep tint indeed.

These photographs show the results of long-term neglect as the cars are left to the ravages of nature. In many cases, it is not possible to judge the model in question, although the make is often discernable due to a portion of radiator shell, wing line or the curve of a roof or boot lid.

This is the Black Museum of the car restorers' world, the place from which there is no return. Whatever material a car's components were made from, they came from the earth. Wood and rubber, glass and metals from sand or rock, and carpets and leather from animal stock. In a few years more, all these materials, with the exception of glass will have corroded, oxidised, rotted or perished. Dust to dust, earth to earth – nature will have had her way.

Right: c.1935 Austin 12
The tombstone-like radiator shell celebrates the car's last resting place on the Isle of Skye.

Above Left: c.1962 Morris 1000 Traveller
The wood frame of these ever popular estate cars is structural, and when it rots…

Below Left: c.1949 Vauxhall Wyvern
Fresh air does not necessarily do you good, if you are a car.

Right: 1919 Buick
Shown as found at the base of Mount Majuba in Natal, South Africa, this Buick looks much the same as a carcass after the lions have finished with it.

Above Left: c.1930 Alvis
Even on a cold winter's morning, the Alvis could tempt a
would-be restorer, but how much has been lost and how deep
is the rust?

Above Right: c.1929 MG M Type
MG's first small sports car was an immediate success, but this one
now would turn to dust at the slightest stirring of the air. Engine
parts, radiator and one headlamp may be its final testament.

Below Left: c.1958 Austin Healey 100/6
Fenced in and fire damaged, this may be the only vehicle in the
book to be unable to yield anything of value to similar vehicles.

Right: c.1952 Jaguar XK120
'Somewhere in South America' this once proud possession of
plantation owner or politician now languishes amongst the foliage,
the fight against humidity and humanity now lost.

Left: c.1930s Saloons, Medlar's Yard, Norwich
The centre car is a Buick; as for the others,
who can say!

Below Left: c.1950 Humber, Medlar's Yard
Is the Humber a rare convertible or has time taken
its toll on the roof?

Below Right: c.1930s Vauxhall, Medlar's Yard
In a quagmire of desiccated vegetation and motor
cars, only the blue Vauxhall and chrome radiator of
a Wolseley are identifiable.

Right: 1930s cars, Medlar's Yard
This famous yard was nearing closure when
the photograph was taken in October 1999.
Over many years, this medley of thirties motors
has succumbed to wind, rain and seedlings.

Left: c.1935 Austin
A large Austin, 16 or 18hp perhaps has all but sunk beneath late autumn leaves. Medlar's yard 2003.

Above Right: c.1931 Armstrong Siddeley
Backed up by more colourful vans from the 1960s, the tree-crushed Armstrong defiantly shows its cooling fan, reminiscent of a Wright Brothers aeroplane propeller.

Below Left: c.1953 Daimler
A typical Medlar's scene. The 'small' Daimler, Conquest or DB18 perhaps, has been there longer than the tree; however it's a battle the Coventry-built car can never win.

Below Right: c.1938 Buick Sedan
A white whale of a car, this American resident of Medlar's has suffered the ignominy of having a kitchen sink or two thrown on top of it.

Left: c.1939/47 Standard
With little left except a strangely sound radiator shell, this Standard sinks below the brambles and scrap iron, like a drowning man beneath the waves: Medlar's Yard 2003.

Above: c.1940s & 1950s Vauxhalls
A world away from Luton, this field of Vauxhalls was snapped in Bentleigh's Yard, New South Wales, Australia.

Above Right: c.1940s Vauxhalls
More of the same, in the same location as the previous image. A sad view today, but a testament to the number of these cars exported following the Second World War.

Below Right: c.1933 Buick Model 50
However large the car and formidable upon the road, when made of steel and aluminium the same end is inevitable.

Above Left: c.1937 Austin 10 Cabriolet
The cabriolet or opening roof version of the Austin 10 was known as the 'Conway'. Relatively rare today, this one, although well on the way to disintegration, has nevertheless been saved for restoration.

Below Left: c.1936 Standard Flying 9
Swarmed upon by stinging nettles, this car is mechanically complete and retains its chrome work in good condition.

Above Right: c.1935 Lanchester 10hp
Sadly, no one seems to want Lanchesters of the 1930s, even when in fine form. So this one may not even be a parts donor.

Below Right: c.1954 Hillman Huskey
An estate version of the Hillman Minx saloon is being lulled into a false sense of security by Mother Nature.

Below Far Right: c.1947 Standard 14
Robbed of much except the Standard 'waterfall' radiator, this car has become the marker for a small scrap heap.

Above Left: c.1937 Morris 10
Was the body taken off or did it rot away?

Below Left: 1933 Austin 7 saloon
Although exposed to the elements for many years, a surprising number of parts were rescued for use on sister cars.

Below Right: c.1948 Bradford van
The commercial branch of Jowett produced these light vans and estate cars. So many similar vehicles seem to have lost their coachwork prior to abandonment, one wonders if grand ideas of re-bodying were stamped on by reality, and projects were abandoned.

Right: c.1934 Standard 12
Corroded beyond hope, a defiant headlamp remains unbowed.

Above: c.1946 Austin 10
Totally neglected Austins of the period seem to have a propensity for their entire sides to rust away from the main body shell, and this is no exception. Soon this car will look like an exploded diagram from a flat pack furniture store.

Below: c.1950 Lagonda 2.6 Litre
Actually, only a body but this aluminium shell demonstrates how much better the lighter metal lasts than steel. Useful panels could still be salvaged.

Left: c.1939 Rover 12hp, c.1956 Ford Prefect, c.1953 Vauxhall Wyvern
All these three are badly off, but the post-war steel seems to have rusted worst of all.

Above Right: c.1939 Rover
Suffering much more decay than vandalism, this example has been fitted with a makeshift radiator grille. Perhaps do-it-yourself maintenance was this cars nemesis.

Below Right: c.1954 Hillman Husky
Although well on its way back to nature, this Hillman seems to have been left in a lean-to shed. Alas, the shed has faired less well than the vehicle.

Left: c.1934 Austin 10 saloon
Retired to a farm near the Kyle of Lochalsh, Scotland, this family Austin is best left where it is. Another similar car can be glimpsed behind it.

Below Left: c.1934 Austin 10 Tourer
And here it is! The one behind in the previous photograph. The tree marks the spot well, and if left alone, would by now be bending metal as growth took place.

Below: c.1928 Armstrong Siddeley, c1938 Vauxhall
The reverse of the photograph states "Huddled together in timeless eventide, a pre-war Armstrong Siddeley keeps company with a large Vauxhall in 'The Camp' a large dump outside St. Ola on the Isle of Orkney."

Right: c.1933 BSA Peerless Coupé
A moody shot in the early morning mist. Note the intact instrument panel which could be saved for other cars.

Above: 1953 Lanchester Leda Saloon
The 14hp car shows its similarity to the parent company's Daimler models. Just how many years of complete neglect were needed to reach this advanced stage of decay, we can only guess. The Vauxhall next to it has done no better. Close inspection will show both cars to be left-hand drive, not unexpected as they are on the island of Minorca.

Above Left: American Miscellany
All cars of American origin but not in a wrecker's yard in the country of their birth. In fact this yard is in Australia.

Below Left: c.1928 Fiat 509 Saloon
Resting and rusting abroad, the vegetation is lending some cheerful colour to this far-gone Fiat. Note the fabric with holes on the doors' coverings.

Right: c.1934 Riley
Although dismantled, much of the Riley remains. A tantalising hint of its past is revealed by a legend painted on the spare-wheel cover stating that the car had undertaken an 'around the world trip'.

Above Left: c.1933 Hudson Terraplane
To move it would be to destroy it. At least one other car lurks behind, possibly a Standard. A few hours with scythe and axe might reveal all sorts of motoring gems, especially as this is once again Medlar's yard.

Below Left: c.1953 Lanchester LD10
Like a puzzle in a children's book, it is hard to see this camouflaged Lanchester.

Above Right: 1920s Rolls-Royce 20hp
Discovered in a field near Kidderminster, in 1999, just about everything that could be removed has been, however, even the remaining steering column, brake lever and bulkhead are worth saving; and if a complete chassis remains, it might still re-take the road under its own power.

Right: c.1955 Armstrong Siddeley Sapphire
Now almost lost to view, this Sapphire seems to have its windows intact, but has 'broken its back' ahead of the windscreen. Not a yard further will this one roll.

Index

AC 58, 59
AEC 229
Albion 7, 210
Alfa Romeo 23, 125
Allard 125
Alvis 48, 70, 95, 96, 122, 127, 129, 158, 191, 194, 236
Amilcar 61, 120
Angus-Sanderson 7, 61
Armstrong Siddeley 7, 80, 82, 139, 241, 250, 254
Aston Martin 82
Austin 7, 12, 14, 17, 21, 28, 31, 32, 33, 36, 39, 44, 46, 48, 51, 57, 69, 70, 74, 85, 89, 95, 96, 99, 105, 106, 107, 120, 126, 129, 132, 136, 142, 147, 150, 152, 153, 154, 159, 160, 165, 190, 200, 206, 218, 225, 232, 236, 241, 243, 244, 246, 249, 250
Autovia 7
Bean 7
Bedford 186, 209, 212, 218, 221, 223, 225
Bentley 9, 39, 70, 82, 105, 122, 134, 136, 146, 150, 152, 170, 172, 174, 175, 190, 192, 194, 198
BMC (British Motor Corporation) 26, 40, 51, 95, 96, 105, 142, 227
BMW 58, 148, 159, 185
Bristol 58, 82, 229
BSA 7, 39, 51, 166, 251
Bugatti 61, 62, 189
Buick 19, 26, 27, 35, 65, 234, 238, 241, 243, 251
Calcott 7
Chevrolet 28, 72, 130, 209, 218
Chrysler 7, 26, 66, 86, 197
Citroën 27, 32, 46, 92, 120, 122, 148
Crossley 7
Crouch 7
Daimler 17, 28, 74, 159, 166, 178, 197, 216, 241, 252
Delage 197
Dennis 229
DeSoto 66
DKW 39
Dodge 19, 40, 86, 100, 207

Fiat 7, 64, 74, 87, 129, 134, 200, 206, 216, 253
Ford 14, 19, 23, 26, 27, 31, 32, 35, 39, 40, 51, 54, 62, 66, 69, 72, 85, 86, 96, 108, 113, 114, 125, 130, 131, 142, 147, 194, 206, 207, 209, 212, 218, 249
Fordson 54, 96, 206, 209, 225, 226, 227
Healey Silverstone 58
Healey Westland 125
Hillman 14, 21, 66, 76, 102, 105, 131, 132, 138, 157, 245, 249
Hispano-Suiza 185, 190
Horstmann 7
HRG 197
Hudson 19, 150, 254
Humber 26, 28, 31, 65, 66, 85, 114, 122, 130, 138, 150, 152, 157, 218, 238
Hupmobile 40, 85
International 26, 85, 102, 209, 216, 226, 227
Jaguar 9, 17, 23, 28, 54, 57, 82, 108, 131, 136, 197, 200, 236
Jeep 39, 65, 66
Jensen 100
Jowett 14, 39, 70, 113, 138, 246
Lagonda 70, 82, 86, 122, 134, 146, 192, 249
Lanchester 39, 51, 72, 164, 166, 245, 252, 254
Lancia 58, 148, 186
Lincoln 62
Lonsdale 7
Lotus 57, 194
McCormick-Deering 227
Mercedes Benz 26, 27, 100, 125, 146, 180, 185, 186, 197
Mercury 62
Messerschmitt 76
MG 28, 39, 48, 55, 57, 76, 95, 106, 113, 129, 131, 136, 142, 236
Monopole 7
Morris 4, 7, 14, 17, 32, 36, 48, 51, 59, 61, 76, 89, 95, 96, 99, 106, 107, 115, 118, 122, 132, 140, 147, 148, 150, 152, 154, 200, 209, 214, 215, 234, 246

Nuffield 76, 89, 114, 140, 160, 227
Oldsmobile 19, 85
Opel 139
Overland 147
Packard 19, 35, 64, 140, 150, 163, 185
Panhard 92, 105, 178
Peugeot 62, 64, 89, 92, 113, 152, 185
Piccard, Pictet & Cie (Pic Pic) 185
Plymouth 19
Pontiac 7
Regal 7
Renault 17, 57, 182, 209, 216
Riley 7, 51, 58, 106, 107, 108, 114, 122, 125, 140, 146, 158, 160, 165, 166, 253
Rolls-Royce 17, 39, 74, 82, 105, 114, 150, 164, 170, 174, 176, 177, 185, 186, 190, 192, 194, 198, 218, 254
Rootes Group 14, 21, 57, 102, 131, 132, 138, 157
Rover 7, 61, 74, 76, 82, 107, 111, 145, 146, 148, 249
Scammell 223
SGM 7
Simca 87, 129
Singer 7, 14, 21, 72, 102, 129, 136, 158, 197
Standard 4, 14, 17, 21, 28, 31, 36, 51, 55, 57, 69, 87, 96, 126, 130, 159, 164, 165, 170, 174, 175, 197, 200, 225, 226, 227, 243, 244, 245, 246, 254, 258
Storey 7
Sunbeam 21, 57, 102, 131, 138, 162, 180
Triumph 55, 87, 95, 99, 106, 107, 132, 136, 142
Trojan 7
Vanden Plas 96, 105, 170, 192
Vauxhall 21, 23, 40, 54, 113, 152, 190, 212, 234, 238, 249, 250
Volkswagen 58
Willys/Willys-Knight 39, 66, 126, 147, 163
Wolseley 7, 28, 31, 48, 59, 76, 89, 96, 106, 108, 113, 134, 147, 160, 238

Design Ben Gibbs - Motion Design, United Kingdom   **Printer** Star Standard Industries Pte Ltd., Singapore   **Printing Equipment** Four colour litho on Roland Speedmaster   **Inks** Toyochem
Page size 260 mm x 230 mm   **Text paper** 170 gsm Stora Enso Matt Art   **End papers** 140 gsm Woodfree   **Dust jacket** 135 gsm Glossy Art